D0282570

HILLARY CLINTON

Recent Titles in Greenwood Biographies

HILLARY CLINTON

A Biography

Dena B. Levy and Nicole R. Krassas

GREENWOOD BIOGRAPHIES

GREENWOOD PRESS
WESTPORT, CONNECTICUT • LONDON

Library of Congress Cataloging-in-Publication Data

Levy, Dena B.
Hillary Clinton : a biography / Dena B. Levy and Nicole R. Krassas.
    p. cm. — (Greenwood biographies, ISSN 1540–4900)
  Includes bibliographical references and index.
  ISBN–13: 978–0–313–33915–8 (alk. paper)
  1. Clinton, Hillary Rodham. 2. Presidents' spouses—United States—Biography.
3. Legislators—United States—Biography. 4. Women legislators—United
States—Biography. 5. United States. Congress. Senate—Biography. 6. Presidential
candidates—United States—Biography. 7. Women presidential candidates—United
States—Biography. I. Krassas, Nicole R. II. Title.

  E887.C55L49   2008
  973.929092—dc22   2007029581

British Library Cataloguing in Publication Data is available.

Library of Congress Catalog Card Number: 2007029581

ISBN-13: 978–0–313–33915–8
ISSN: 1540–4900

First published in 2008

Greenwood Press, 88 Post Road West, Westport, CT 06881
An imprint of Greenwood Publishing Group, Inc.
www.greenwood.com

Printed in the United States of America

The paper used in this book complies with the
Permanent Paper Standard issued by the National
Information Standards Organization (Z39.48–1984).

10 9 8 7 6 5 4 3 2 1

For Isabel, Maggie, and Anna

CONTENTS

Photo essay follows page 48

SERIES FOREWORD

In response to high school and public library needs, Greenwood developed this distinguished series of full-length biographies specifically for student use. Prepared by field experts and professionals, these engaging biographies are tailored for high school students who need challenging yet accessible biographies. Ideal for secondary school assignments, the length, format and subject areas are designed to meet educators' requirements and students' interests.

Greenwood offers an extensive selection of biographies spanning all curriculum-related subject areas including social studies, the sciences, literature and the arts, history, and politics, as well as popular culture, covering public figures and famous personalities from all time periods and backgrounds, both historic and contemporary, who have made an impact on American and/or world culture. Greenwood biographies are chosen based on comprehensive feedback from librarians and educators. Consideration is given to both curriculum relevance and inherent interest. The result is an intriguing mix of the well known and the unexpected, the saints and sinners from long-ago history and contemporary pop culture. Readers will find a wide array of subject choices from fascinating crime figures like Al Capone to inspiring pioneers like Margaret Mead, from the greatest minds of our time like Stephen Hawking to the most amazing success stories of our day like J. K. Rowling.

While the emphasis is on fact, not glorification, the books are meant to be fun to read. Each volume provides in-depth information about the subject's life from birth through childhood, the teen years, and adulthood.

A thorough account relates family background and education, traces personal and professional influences, and explores struggles, accomplishments, and contributions. A timeline highlights the most significant life events against a historical perspective. Bibliographies supplement the reference value of each volume.

INTRODUCTION

Writing about a public figure like Hillary Rodham Clinton provides some unique challenges. While many in the political realm manage to fly under the radar, Senator Clinton seems to be a magnet for attention. Even dating back to her college days she made news. While her childhood was relatively uneventful and even emblematic of suburban America, little about her since she graduated from college has remained so. Indeed, she is one of the best-known women in American politics, and even around the world. Quite simply, Senator Clinton makes and sells news. This public prominence translates into telling a story about someone whom the public believes they already know. Yet there is always more to learn, and oftentimes what we think we know may not be true.

Hillary Clinton is a lightning rod; there are few people without some kind of opinion already formed about her. There are those who admire her for all she has accomplished and those who strongly dislike her either for her presumed ideological positions or for staying with her husband despite his cheating. Yet how well does the public really know Mrs. Clinton? While she has had a very public career, she remains a very private individual. The constant scrutiny by the press into the lives of her and her husband has created a woman who distrusts the media and fails to use them to her advantage. Moreover, her upbringing taught her self-reliance and the value of self-containment. Unlike many in our culture of exposure, Hillary Clinton does not want to publicly bare her inner life.

While a multitude of books have been written about Senator Clinton in which she has received her share of both positive and negative coverage, this particular book takes a different approach. As political scientists we use our discipline to set the framework for telling the story of her life. This allows us to examine the various events, activities, and accomplishments of Hillary Clinton in a unique manner. Political science tells us about the role of socialization in shaping the viewpoints of individuals, about the types of activities in which members of Congress engage, and how presidential elections are shaped by the primary system. It is important to consider these theories and others to understand how Mrs. Clinton has become such an important person in our political arena.

The book follows Clinton's life in chronological order. Chapter 1 begins with the story of her parents and then moves to her own childhood. Chapter 2 finds Hillary Rodham in college and law school. Chapter 3 shifts to her years in Arkansas, while chapter 4 centers on the 1992 election campaign. Chapters 5 and 6 discuss Mrs. Clinton's time in the White House with her husband, President Clinton. Chapter 7 provides insight into Senator Clinton's congressional career, while chapter 8 covers the 2008 presidential campaign.

Hopefully, the unique approach taken in this book will provide the reader with insight into the "true" Hillary Clinton. She is an incredibly smart and talented woman who has borne the brunt of public scrutiny for most of her adult life. The public and the media have not always been fair to her, yet she has also made inopportune decisions that have backfired and exacerbated the sometimes unflattering way in which she is viewed. While Clinton is not perfect and is indeed a politician, she is without question someone who has served her country well, from adolescence to adulthood.

TIMELINE: EVENTS IN THE LIFE OF HILLARY CLINTON

October 26, 1947	Hillary Rodham born
1965	Graduated from high school
1969	Graduated from Wellesley College
1973	Graduated from Yale University Law School
1973–1974	Worked on impeachment trials of President Richard Nixon
1975	Joined University of Arkansas Law School faculty
1975	Married William Jefferson Clinton
1976	Joined the Rose Law Firm
1978	Appointed by President Jimmy Carter to the board of Legal Services Corporation
1979	Made full partner at Rose Law Firm (first woman to do so)
1980	Birth of daughter, Chelsea
1982–1992	First Lady, state of Arkansas
1982	Began using the name Hillary Rodham Clinton
1983	Named Arkansas woman of the year
1984	Named Arkansas mother of the year
1985–1992	Served on board of directors for Wal-Mart and for TCBY
1988 and 1991	Named 1 of 100 most influential lawyers in the country (by National Law Journal)
1992–2000	First Lady, United States of America

1993	Chaired task force on national health care reform
1995	Publication of *It Takes a Village*
2001–present	U.S. senator, State of New York
2003	Publication of memoir *Living History*
January 20, 2007	Establishes exploratory committee to consider running for president in 2008

Chapter 1

FAMILY ROOTS

In January 2007, the field of presidential candidates for the Democratic Party had already grown to eight individuals—one of those, Hillary Clinton, is set to make history should she be selected as the eventual nominee. If she succeeds in winning the primary election, she would likely be considered the most viable woman presidential candidate in the United States, with a true chance of winning the general election. But this is not Senator Clinton's first "first" success. Hillary Rodham Clinton is arguably one of the most recognizable political figures throughout much of the world. She has led a career with many ups and downs but has always forged ahead to pursue her goals, breaking down barriers along the way. A child coming of age in the 1960s, she has been shaped by the turbulent times in which she grew up—and she has landed in places that she probably could not have dreamt of. She is a First Lady who became a U.S. senator and is now on the brink of becoming the Democratic nominee for president of the United States. The story of Hillary Clinton is one of hard work, intelligence, diligence, and a little bit of luck. It is a political tale that has long intrigued the public. Over the next two years, that story will continue to unfold as she runs for the highest elective office in the land. But in order to understand where she is now, it is necessary to understand where she started.

As is the case for many of us, our childhood foundation lays roots that remain with us throughout our lives. Such is the case for Hillary Rodham Clinton. Her childhood experiences and influences shaped the woman she is today. In Senator Clinton's case, two men played a critical role in her development, ironically pulling her in opposite directions. However,

Hillary Clinton's story begins with that of her parents, as their childhoods left a distinct impression on her own development.

Hillary Clinton's father, Hugh E. Rodham, grew up in Scranton, Pennsylvania. A son of a supervisor at the Scranton Lace Company, it was assumed that Rodham would also work in the lace business. Very much a middle child, Rodham grew up believing that he was lacking in the qualities that his two brothers possessed. His older brother, Willard, was the responsible one, while his younger brother, Russell, was the smart and successful one. In contrast, Hugh was the brother who was often in trouble, misbehaving in church or joyriding.[1] Hugh accepted his fate of working in the lace mill, but he was ultimately spared when his best friend was recruited to play football at Penn State and would attend only if Rodham also played. As a result, Rodham attended college, played football, and received his degree in physical education. Upon graduation, rather than returning to Scranton, Rodham hopped a freight train and landed in Chicago, where he got a job selling curtains. This was in 1935, during the Great Depression. Although his mother, Hannah Rodham, was not pleased that her son left Pennsylvania, Rodham's job helped to support his family during the financial crisis. Eventually, Rodham parlayed his experience as a traveling salesman and his knowledge of fabric into his own business making curtains for hotels, banks, and offices. On his own he managed every aspect of the job—buying the fabric, sewing the curtains, delivering them, and even hanging them up.[2] His self-discipline and self-reliance were character traits instilled into his own children. They grew up knowing that their father valued the ability to succeed on one's own merits; after all, that was precisely what he himself had done. Given his background, the unexpected opportunity for him to attend college, and then the success of owning his own business, it is not surprising to hear Hugh Rodham described as a tough task master, one who very much valued education.

Hillary's mother, Dorothy Howell Rodham, had a more harrowing childhood. She was essentially abandoned by her mother by the age of three or four and forced to largely fend for herself with her father and younger sister. By the time that Dorothy was eight, her parents had divorced, and her father no longer felt capable of taking care of her and her younger sister, Isabelle. Dorothy and Isabelle were sent out to their paternal grandmother, Emma Howell, via train from Illinois to California, unaccompanied. Unfortunately for them, Emma Howell was a strict and harsh woman, ill prepared to have young children in her care. Dorothy spent six years under her roof. One story from Dorothy's childhood particularly exemplifies the difficult circumstances in which she was raised.

Dorothy went trick-or-treating with friends from school, but Emma Howell disapproved and responded by punishing her granddaughter and confining her to her bedroom for a year, except during school hours. Dorothy was not even allowed to eat with the rest of the family. Fortunately, Dorothy's great-aunt visited and put an end to the harsh punishment.[3]

Eventually, Dorothy decided to leave her grandparent's home to become an au pair. Living for the first time, at the age of 14, among a close-knit family provided Dorothy with a role model that she would later draw upon when raising her own family. Indeed, this experience proved crucial to Dorothy Rodham's eventual role as mother herself. Without the time spent as an au pair, Dorothy might never have experienced what it was to be in a loving family environment. Dorothy intended to remain in California to attend college, but upon being contacted by her long-absent mother, she returned to Chicago. Excited at the prospect of reuniting with her mother, she was soon disappointed to learn that her mother wanted her only to serve as a housekeeper. Dorothy's dreams of both a warm reconciliation with her mother and of attending college faded away, and she instead found an office job and her own apartment. While disappointing, these events proved critical to the story of Dorothy's daughter, Hillary, for it was in Chicago that Dorothy Howell met and eventually married Hugh Rodham.

Dorothy Howell's and Hugh Rodham's paths crossed when Howell applied for a job at a textile company. They dated for several years and married in 1942. They began their lives together in a small apartment in Lincoln Park, Chicago. Hillary Rodham was born in Chicago on October 26, 1947, followed by her two brothers, Hugh and Tony. Eventually, Hugh Rodham's business became sufficiently successful to support the family moving to the conservative suburb of Park Ridge, where Hillary Rodham would grow up influenced by the homogeneity of her neighborhood. Hugh Rodham did not believe in credit, so the family did not move out of their one-bedroom apartment until he had the $21,000 in cash needed to purchase their Park Ridge home.[4]

PARK RIDGE

Park Ridge was known as a middle-class neighborhood with little diversity in either demographics or worldviews. It was a predominantly white, middle-class community with parents, who were mostly politically conservative, commuting to Chicago for their jobs. Located under the flight path of Chicago's busy O'Hare airport, Park Ridge was otherwise the idyllic suburb with tree-lined streets and comfortable homes. Interestingly,

Park Ridge would later be the home of conservative Republican Henry Hyde, who spent a considerable portion of his career in the U.S. House of Representatives fighting abortion rights. Conservative still today, Park Ridge was then a community where families left their doors unlocked and children were able to play in the streets. Until 1980, Park Ridge was a dry community (that is, the sale of alcohol was banned), and when Hillary was growing up, it was the second-most Republican town in America.[5]

Communities such as Park Ridge still exist today, though no doubt far fewer than during Hillary's childhood. They are, nonetheless, recognizable for their homogeneity. Neighbors resemble one another in outlook and experiences. Individuals out of step with the prevailing norms may feel disconnected. In the 1950s, when Hillary was growing up, middle-class mothers tended to remain at home, while fathers worked to support their families. It was a stereotypical suburban childhood, and Hillary's childhood is more notable for its ordinariness than anything else.[6]

HILLARY'S CHILDHOOD

Hugh Rodham was conservative not only in his politics but also in his approach to child rearing. Family outings sometimes consisted of Hugh driving Hillary and her brothers past Chicago's skid row, where he would point out what happens to people who lack self-discipline and adequate motivation. He was extremely strict and frequently found his children lacking in their endeavors. When Hillary received a report card with all As, her father's only response was that the school must not be very difficult if she were doing so well. Fortunately, Hillary's response to her father's apparent criticism was to view it as a challenge to do even better on the next assignment. As an adult looking back on her childhood, she appreciated what she viewed as her father encouraging her to work as hard as possible because the world was a tough place and success required hard work.[7] Of course, other children might have crumbled under such an approach, but it clearly worked for Hillary Rodham. Rather than folding, she continued to rise to her father's challenges and, as a result, excelled in most aspects of her life.

Her quest to succeed was not limited to academics; she strived to be the best at everything she tried, regardless of natural aptitude. This desire stemmed in part from the expectations placed on her, and her brothers, by her demanding father. The area beyond Hillary's innate talents was sports. However, her father placed considerable value on athleticism, and although Hillary was not particularly gifted in this area, her father worked with her every Sunday to ensure that she could eventually "hit a decent softball. Decent, but not great."[8] Despite her difficulties in sports, she played softball throughout the summers of high school and demonstrated the characteristic many see in her even today—the persistence to continue when faced with seemingly insurmountable challenges. Hillary also played tennis and volleyball, swam, and learned ballet.

Hillary was always an outstanding student who is fondly remembered by many of her teachers for the quality of her work and her curiosity to learn. She was known in her school as one of the best students, yet she managed to be fairly popular among her peers. And when neighborhood children bullied her as the new kid in town, Hillary proved to be capable of defending herself thanks to encouragement from her mother. When Hillary went home to complain to her mother about being hit, her mother told her she needed to stand up for herself: "There's no room in this house for cowards."[9] The next time a neighborhood girl tried to push her around, Hillary punched her in the nose; she never had problems with the kids in her neighborhood again and even became good friends with the girl who hit her.

Hillary Rodham filled her childhood with numerous events, activities, and endeavors. Even at a young age, she organized those around her. As a Brownie and then a Girl Scout, she participated in the multitude of activities stemming from those organizations, such as bake sales, parades, and efforts to obtain merit badges. One of her nonacademic activities noted by many biographers was her role as a Girl Scout. She was remembered by teachers as a girl who often proudly wore her Girl Scout uniform to school with all its badges and awards displayed.

Her interest in helping others began at a young age when she would organize neighborhood carnivals and sporting events, often to raise money for charities.[10] She also loved sports and was a big baseball fan, rooting for the Chicago Cubs. As she would explain many years later when running for the Senate, she was also a fan of the New York Yankees because it would have been considered sacrilegious to root for the White Sox, the Chicago team that was part of the American League. As a candidate for Senate, Hillary Clinton explained that her love of the Yankees stemmed from her childhood, but many New Yorkers were skeptical and viewed her explanations as politically motivated.

Hillary was strongly influenced by her opinionated father and was very conservative in her outlook. According to one biographer, Gail Sheehy, Hillary viewed the world in black and white with little gray in between.[11] In part this was due to the influence of a father who thought in terms of absolutes. He conveyed his attitude to his daughter and taught her that Republicans were good and Democrats were bad. Hugh Rodham was such

a strong Republican supporter that when John F. Kennedy beat Richard
Nixon for the presidency, Hillary was concerned about the legitimacy of
the election and volunteered to go to Chicago to try to determine whether
the election was fraudulent.[12] She and a friend, Betsy Johnson, went to
Chicago without permission and volunteered with a group of Republicans
to check voter lists against addresses to attempt to uncover voter fraud.
Amazingly, each girl was given a list of names, and they were separated
into different groups with strangers and then dropped off alone in unfamiliar neighborhoods. Hillary ended up in a poor neighborhood in the
South Side of Chicago, where she naively went about the business of trying to uncover voter fraud. While she did discover a vacant lot and a bar
listed as the home addresses of several voters, she also went to numerous
homes and woke up many people who either "stumbled to the door or
yelled at [her] to go away."[13] When she eventually returned home, she
proudly reported to her father that she found evidence of the voter fraud
that he decried. Rodham, however, was less concerned with the Kennedy
victory than the fact that his daughter had wandered around the South
Side unaccompanied by an adult.[14]

While Hillary would eventually view the world in more shades of gray,
she seems to maintain even today a tendency toward absolutes instilled
by her father. Her later relationship with the media while First Lady was
colored by her tendency to see them as a single entity in a negative light.
Yet Hillary's mother also influenced her with a more moderate approach
to the world. Mrs. Rodham was essentially a Democrat in her political
outlook but rarely declared her views in the vocal manner of her husband.
As a result, it was Hugh Rodham's political views that were more overtly
expressed than those of Mrs. Rodham. Hillary Clinton's mother, however,
ensured that Hillary grew up participating in many activities, such as taking dance and music lessons. She also encouraged her daughter to read
and pushed her to believe that she could do anything she wanted. The
Rodhams instilled in their daughter the dual belief that education for the
sake of education was critical, but that education would provide opportunities that would not otherwise be available.[15] Dorothy Rodham was
not able to go to college, but wanted to ensure that her daughter was not
deprived of that opportunity. Mrs. Rodham also felt strongly that Hillary
should not grow up spoiled. To that end, Hillary and her two brothers
were expected to help around the house doing chores, and none were paid
to do so.[16] As was typical of the middle-class husbands and wives of their
generation, Mrs. Rodham focused on the home life, while Mr. Rodham
brought in the news from the outside world.[17]

Interestingly, a pivotal moment in young Hillary's life was the space race with Russia. Hillary was devastated to learn that the Russians were able to beat the Americans at putting a satellite, Sputnik, into space. As a result, Hillary's first ambition was to study science and work to help the Americans catch up. She then decided to become an astronaut and was crushed to learn that NASA only trained men for that job. While Hillary rarely felt doors close to her because of her sex, this was one instance in which she was clearly disadvantaged simply by virtue of being female. Hillary was later able to console herself with the knowledge that her poor eyesight would have ultimately precluded her from becoming an astronaut, if her sex hadn't.

While many people today may not agree with Hillary Clinton's politics, few question her intelligence. So it was when she was a young student. When in high school, Hillary excelled in most of her subjects. She also participated in extracurricular activities. As a junior, she was vice president of her class, and the next year, she was a senior leader—essentially an assistant teacher. She was also the chair of the school organization committee, requiring her to run the 2,700-member student-body school assemblies. Hillary graduated in the top 5 percent of her class and was presciently voted the girl most likely to succeed. Clearly, her classmates were able to recognize even then the potential of Hillary Rodham. Hillary was also popular among her peers, with both the boys and girls. However, she did not understand why some of her girlfriends became so preoccupied with attracting boys that that they allowed their grades to slip. Hillary did not let that happen to her; not until she met her future husband did a man seem to intrude upon her own ambitions. In 1964, she surprised the entire high school by putting in her name as a candidate for class president. No female student in the history of the school had ever before run for the office. Hillary was beaten badly by the captain of the football team, but she put on a courageous campaign. She made well-prepared speeches and outdebated her opponent but lost anyway in a race that was more about star quality and personality than about qualifications.

One of Hillary's most frustrating memories from high school was being given an assignment to role-play for a debate between Goldwater and Johnson. Her teacher knew that Hillary was strongly supportive of Goldwater and that her fellow student in the assignment preferred Johnson. He thus assigned Hillary to play Johnson and her fellow student to play Goldwater. Both girls were furious about their assignments, and Hillary hated having to learn about the Johnson administration. She already felt she knew enough about it and that playing Johnson was unfair to her beliefs. The pedagogical rationale behind the assignment was lost on the politically rigid Hillary. At the time, Hillary was not shaken in her conservative convictions by this experience, though, ironically, by the time the two young women graduated from college, each had switched her partisanship.

The beginning of the moderation of Hillary's politics came at the hands of her youth minister, Donald Jones. Raised as a Methodist, Hillary was active in her church. When Jones was hired, he created a program called "University of Life," in which he took his students outside of their safe, sterile life and exposed them to the world beyond their sheltered suburb. He took them on tours of the inner city of Chicago and organized meetings with inner-city gang youths, and he took them to see Martin Luther King Jr. speak and to meet him afterward. According to Hillary Clinton herself, because of Reverend Jones she "first read [poets] e. e. cummings and T. S. Eliot; experienced Picasso's paintings, especially *Guernica*, and debated the meaning of the "Grand Inquisitor" in Dostoyevsky's *Brothers Karamazov*."[18] Going to museums, reading books that challenged her, and meeting with youth groups from Chicago's inner city all helped plant the seeds of what would later become Hillary's conversion to the Democratic Party. Don Jones provided Hillary with the first glimpse of a world that was very different from her own. She discovered that while the experiences of some of the black and Hispanic youths she met were different from hers, what they shared in common outweighed the differences. In addition, she realized that many of these young students were better informed about the civil rights movement than she was at the time. She only knew a little about Rosa Parks and Dr. King but was intrigued when learning more from the exchange sessions.[19] These insights were fundamental in shaping her future views, which continue to play out today. In fact, it may be possible to see the seeds of Hillary's future interest in children's welfare in her high school experience. While she was intrigued and excited by the new experiences brought to her attention, Hillary was not yet ready to walk away from the Park Ridge worldview.

At the same time that Hillary was being drawn into Jones's University of Life curriculum, she joined the anti-Communist club of her history teacher, Paul Carlson, and attended its secret meetings. Neither Carlson nor Jones knew of her involvement in the other's program. The dichotomy of experience and attitudes presented to her by both men was remarkable. While Jones introduced Hillary to abstract art, Beat poetry, and Martin Luther King Jr., Carlson was bringing in military or extreme conservative speakers to talk to his group. However, Hillary didn't believe the views of Carlson and Jones to be that different from one another and did not recognize at the time the tremendous conflict that existed between the two men. According to Jones, he and Carlson were "locked in a battle for [Hillary's] mind and soul."[20]

The safety and shelter of Hillary's childhood cannot be overstated. There was little diversity of opinion or outlook in her upbringing; most of the families in her community looked at the world in the same way, and there were few voices challenging the status quo of the time. Eventually Jones's activities started generating concern among the conservative parents of Park Ridge. Paul Carlson was among those opposed to Jones's activities, including the University of Life curriculum, and he also pushed for Jones's removal from the church. After only two years, Jones ultimately opted to leave his position as youth minister at the First Methodist Church to take a position at Drew University, where he remained until finally retiring as professor emeritus of social ethics. However, his impact lasted with Hillary, and they maintained a letter-writing relationship that continued into her adulthood. It is clear that Don Jones served as the counterbalance to Hugh Rodham in shaping Hillary's outlook. Although she continued to strive to please her father, she could not ignore the lessons being taught to her by her youth minister. By virtue of leaving the closed community of Park Ridge and being exposed to the inner city of Chicago, Hillary observed firsthand the vast disparities in experiences of individuals from different walks of life.

The impact of Hugh Rodham also cannot be overstated. It is not unusual for a daughter to be influenced by her father, and Hillary is no exception. He had high expectations for his children, and he often found them lacking. Perhaps one could make the case that Rodham set the foundation for Hillary to put others first when it came to her own ambitions. Although she was clearly an outstanding student, Hugh Rodham rarely demonstrated his pride in her achievements in an overt manner. His lack of praise for her accomplishments prevented Hillary from becoming a self-centered know-it-all. Instead, she was valued more for her hard work on behalf of others than for focusing only on herself. Yet while he may not have been vocal about his pride in his daughter, it is notable that Hugh Rodham selected a town with high property taxes to support education. He believed that education was critical and often assisted Hillary with her studying, particularly in math.

Eventually, Hillary needed to select a college. Although she originally assumed she would stay in the Midwest, she was fortunate that two of her teachers took an interest in her future and suggested she look at Wellesley and Smith colleges. They argued that attending a women's college would allow Hillary to focus on her studies during the week and then play on weekends. Although she attended alumnae events in Chicago for both colleges and felt out of place (the other women attending the parties seemed more worldly to Hillary), she was accepted to both and chose Wellesley based on the campus pictures. Her parents drove her to Wellesley, just outside of Boston and dropped her off at the college where she would eventually change her party affiliation, become a political activist, and ultimately shape her future. The year was 1965.

NOTES

1. Hillary Rodham Clinton, *Living History* (New York: Simon and Schuster, 2003).

2. Gail Sheehy, *Hillary's Choice* (New York: Random House, 1999).

3. Hillary Rodham Clinton, *Living History* (New York: Simon and Schuster, 2003).

4. Helen Kennedy, "The Girl Who Became Hillary," *New York Daily News*, February 6, 2000.

5. Ibid.

6. Nancy Benac, "Hillary Clinton's Life of Improbable Turns Pivots Again," *Associated Press*, January 21, 2007.

7. Judith Warner, *Hillary Clinton: The Inside Story* (New York: Penguin Books, 1993).

8. Ibid., p. 25.

9. Gail Sheehy, *Hillary's Choice* (New York: Random House, 1999), p. 24.

10. Hillary Rodham Clinton, *Living History* (New York: Simon and Schuster, 2003).

11. Ibid.

12. Ibid., p. 7.

13. Ibid., p. 17.

14. Ibid.

15. Judith Warner, *Hillary Clinton: The Inside Story* (New York: Penguin Books, 1993).

16. Ibid.

17. Ibid.

18. Ibid., p. 22.

19. Ibid.

20. Ibid., p. 23.

Chapter 2

COLLEGE YEARS AND
LAW SCHOOL

If growing up in Park Ridge helped to shape Hillary Rodham's once-conservative leanings, it was her college years that ultimately completed the transition initiated by Donald Jones' University of Life classes. College for Hillary Rodham was, as is the case for many, extremely influential in shaping her political views and career aspirations.

Political socialization is an area of fascination for many political scientists. Scholars interested in this subfield attempt to answer the question of how we form the opinions and views that make us believe what we do. In other words, how do we become Democrats and Republicans, liberals and conservatives, activists and bystanders? From where do we learn our worldviews? For most of us, there are a multitude of influences on our beliefs, ranging from our family to our peers to our teachers to the media. The relative influence of each of these varies with the greatest contributing influence—usually the family. One definition of political socialization is "the process by which people acquire the values, beliefs, and opinions that motivate their involvement and condition their activities in the political system."[1]

The family is an obvious agent of socialization because of the sheer number of hours that children spend with at least one family member. The degree to which a child will be influenced by his or her family depends to some extent on the salience of politics in the household. Thus, a family in which politics is rarely discussed will probably not exert the same impact as one in which the topic of politics is commonly addressed. Hillary Rodham's family would have been an important source of her earliest political views; her father's influence would have been especially important since he was the more vocal parent when it came to discussing politics. While her mother impacted other areas of Hillary's childhood, it was her father's absolutist conservative views that were transmitted to her. In addition, Hillary has credited her father with instilling in her the importance of defending her convictions. Later in life, Hugh Rodham would joke with his daughter that allowing her to go to Wellesley had been a "great miscalculation," given her ideological shift in college.[2]

School, and in particular teachers, also played an important role in Hillary Rodham's political development. While the research shows a weak, if any, specific relationship between school and the political socialization of an individual, there does seem to be evidence indicating that school reflects the broader environment in which a student is raised.[3] Thus, a school in a conservative suburb such as Park Ridge will generally reflect the core values of the community. That is certainly the case for Hillary Rodham's academic experience through high school. In fact, only the youth minister of her church struck a discordant note in terms of reflecting the conservative nature of the neighborhood. It should be noted that at least one of Hillary's teachers wanted to expose her to different political views with the Johnson role-playing assignment, but it is likely that the assignment was a pedagogical tool as opposed to any particular effort to dissuade Hillary from her political views. Most of her teachers were content to support the conservative outlook of the community.

Hillary Rodham was a reflection of her politically conservative community until she left to attend Wellesley College. While the seeds of a more liberal outlook were planted by the interaction with her youth minister and his attempts to broaden the experiences of his students, it was at college that Hillary increasingly began to reflect on the world in a different way than she had during her childhood. The effect of major events in society cannot be overestimated as an independent factor shaping an individual's political views. This is the case with the Vietnam War and the civil rights movement for Hillary Rodham. These events, and others of the time, had profound effects on her continuing political socialization. However, it was not just events of the day that influenced Hillary. In her freshman year, she worked in a tutoring program for inner-city youths. Seeing the lives of poor children up close had a profound effect on her political outlook, according to her youth minister, Don Jones.[4] This experience continued her exposure to individuals with different backgrounds, which was first begun by Jones in his University of Life program during Hillary's high school years.

For Hillary Rodham, Wellesley was a transformative experience. Attending a women's college during the tumultuous 1960s was liberating in many ways. Vietnam, the civil rights movement, the assassinations of Martin Luther King Jr. and Robert Kennedy Jr. all had an impact on Hillary's outlook. Following her commitment to Republican politics and her sash-wearing support for Barry Goldwater, Hillary jumped right into activities on the Wellesley campus. During her freshman year, she was president of the college's Young Republicans. In 1966, she worked for the senate campaign of Republican Edward Brooke, who became the first black senator since Reconstruction. Hillary urged her fellow students to get involved in any way they felt comfortable, calling on them to volunteer to do office work if the more public acts of campaigning were too onerous. Throughout her time at Wellesley, Hillary was frenetically involved in all kinds of campus activities. One college roommate noted that Hillary started out "involved in everything" but realized that at some point she would have to make a choice.[5] As a political science major, Hillary's choices focused mainly on political issues. She was also focused on doing what it took to become a lawyer.

It was at Wellesley that Hillary finally came into her own, both as an academic and as a politician. She ultimately ran for class president, and unlike her experience in high school when she ran for senior class president and lost, she was victorious. She influenced many of her classmates, who knew that turning to Hillary meant that a perceived problem or challenge would be met and addressed. While many college students in the later part of the 1960s focused a great deal of their attention on events in the world, Hillary focused her attention on issues at Wellesley, including pass-fail grading, fewer course requirements, greater enrollment of blacks, and a college-prep program for inner-city youths. Her interest in the college-prep program stemmed directly from her early experiences as a tutor in Boston.

Hillary's political activities were not limited to the campus. She participated in a number of local and national marches in support of political causes. An emotional Hillary Rodham even donned a black armband to march in solidarity with other mourners after the assassination of Martin Luther King Jr. in 1968. That summer, Hillary told her parents she was off to the movies and instead took the train to downtown Chicago with an old friend in order to see the demonstrations of mostly antiwar protestors outside of the Democratic National Convention. The ensuing riots left a profound impact on the young women who had never been witness to that sort of violence.[6]

Hillary and her classmates attended Wellesley during a truly transformative period. Hillary's life in Illinois had prepared her to pursue a career in public service. Her experience at Wellesley prepared her to make that career in a way that women had not typically considered. Traditionally, women attending Wellesley were getting a college education but were also looking for their future husbands. Indeed, Wellesley had in place in loco parentis regulations that required parental permission for students to leave the college boundaries. However, during the time that Hillary was a student at the college, these regulations and some required courses deemed by the students to be unnecessary were eliminated, in part due to Hillary's own efforts as class president. By the time that Hillary and her classmates graduated, the college had completed its transformation from hunting grounds for husband material to a top-notch college graduating some of the best and brightest women in the country. Hillary completed the transition by becoming the first student allowed to speak at graduation. Students demanded to hear from one of their own about their college experiences. While the college administration was initially opposed to opening up the podium to a student, they eventually relented, in part because they knew that Hillary would be the speaker. She assured them that she would give an address appropriate for the occasion. However, she surprised even herself by straying from her prepared text to respond directly to the comments of the speaker preceding her, Senator Edward Brooke, whom she campaigned for during her freshman year. Her resulting address criticized Brooke, Congress, the presidential administration, and the public for not being bold enough and for not seeking solutions to issues of the time. In her speech, she argued that the people of her generation were seeking something new:

> We are, all of us, exploring a world that none of us even understands and attempting to create within that uncertainty. But there are some things we feel, feelings that our prevailing, acquisitive, and competitive corporate life, including tragically the universities, is not the way of life for us. We're searching for more immediate, ecstatic and penetrating mode of living. And so our questions, our questions about our institutions, about our colleges, about our churches, about our government continue. The questions about those institutions are familiar to all of us.... Senator Brooke has suggested some of them this morning. But along with using these words—integrity, trust, and respect—in regard to institutions and leaders we're perhaps harshest with them in regard to ourselves.[7]

Hillary's speech was sufficiently notable that she, along with Ira Magaziner (student speaker at Brown University), was featured in *Life* magazine.

Her only family member to witness the famous speech was Hugh Rodham, who made the trip in his signature Cadillac to see his daughter embark on her own American dream. In keeping with the times, the *Life* picture showed Hillary as a young woman wearing her signature thick glasses and a determined look on her face.

Perhaps the most telling indicator of the depth to which her talk rattled the college administration occurred when the college president asked a groundskeeper to steal Hillary's clothes and glasses, which she left lying on the banks of the lake while taking a post-graduation swim![8] In her 1992 commencement speech at Wellesley, Hillary remarked that she was glad no one had pictures of her trying, with her poor vision, to find her way back to her dorm in her bathing suit.

Hillary continued her exposure to the volatile world of politics in the 1960s by partaking in a Wellesley internship program in Washington, D.C. After some initial reluctance, her advisor placed her with the House Republican Conference to help her continue to determine her political perspective. During this internship, she attended the 1968 Republican Convention in Miami, working for the Rockefeller campaign. This experience was to be later juxtaposed to the Democratic Convention, which was held in Chicago. When Hillary was back home from her summer internship, she and a friend were in Grant Park and saw firsthand the riots that took place as frustrated antiwar demonstrators responded to the Democratic Convention. The year 1968 was a watershed for many who were old enough to be aware of what was happening in American politics. Hillary was no exception: "I did not imagine then that I would ever run for office, but I knew I wanted to participate as both a citizen and an activist."[9]

Her interest in activism was cemented by her senior thesis in which she wrote about Saul Alinsky, a radical community organizer in Chicago. Hillary met Alinsky as a high school student when she participated in the University of Life program. Hillary met him at the same time that she met Reverend Martin Luther King Jr. When trying to decide on a topic for her senior thesis, her college advisor suggested that she recontact Alinsky and write about him.[10] Interestingly, Hillary Rodham's thesis would become a topic of discussion and interest far into the future when she was First Lady. In 1993, at the request of the Clintons, Wellesley College made an unusual decision to file the thesis away and not allow anyone to read it— particularly those who would be writing President Clinton's biographies. Needless to say, the decision to put the thesis under lock and key while the Clintons were in the White House led to considerable speculation about the content. Today, the thesis is available to anyone who makes the trip to the Wellesley library archives.[11] Although Alinsky ended up offering Hillary a job working for his organization, she ultimately decided to attend law school. Hillary knew she wanted to make a difference in society; the only question was whether to do so from the inside or outside. Alinsky's approach was to push from the outside using activist techniques. Ultimately, Hillary decided to attend Yale University Law School in order to achieve her goal of changing society, thereby deciding on the inside approach to making changes. Hillary's decision to attend law school is in keeping with many of the choices she has made throughout her life. She follows rules and seems more comfortable with conventional choices. Also, she fundamentally believes that working for change from the inside is the best method for enduring success.

After leaving Wellesley in 1969, Hillary spent the summer in Alaska, where she traveled about, working whatever jobs she could find. While working in a fish cannery, Hillary found herself fired for doing exactly what she was praised for at Wellesley, speaking her mind. The owner of the cannery apparently took offense when Hillary pointed out that the fish looked discolored and unfit for human consumption. Little else is known about her trip to Alaska, except that she was able to earn enough money to get back East and move into the law school dorms at Yale.[12]

Despite her ambition, Hillary wasn't immune to romantic interests. Although in her own memoir she mentions that she dated throughout college, she doesn't particularly mention any one man over another. Hillary's college friends note that while she was not especially concerned with dating and socializing during college, she could be counted on to have fun and add life to any gathering. Most of the young men she dated seem to have shared her political convictions. In an interview with the *Daily News*, a former boyfriend, Geoffrey Shields, commented that she was most animated when discussing political issues. However, according to Gail Sheehy's book *Hillary's Choice*, Hillary had a very serious boyfriend prior to the entrance of Bill Clinton into her life. According to Sheehy, Hillary met David Rupert while interning in Washington and subsequently dated him through her second year of law school. Interestingly, among the myriad of other works written about Hillary, none has mentioned this relationship.[13] According to Sheehy, Rupert and Hillary ultimately broke up due to differences in long-term goals and, perhaps, because Bill Clinton had entered the picture, and Hillary found in him someone she simply did not want to live without.

It is clear that Hillary Clinton is who she is in part because of the combination of the college she attended and the times during which she attended. In other words, for Hillary, attending a women's college was liberating, allowing her to pursue her academic achievements without fear of alienating potential boyfriends. She found it empowering to realize that women were in charge of everything from the school newspaper to the student government. In addition, the period in which she attended college was one of the most politically influential for an entire generation. The combination of Vietnam, her involvement with the poor in Boston, and the assassinations of Robert Kennedy and Martin Luther King Jr. caused her to emerge from her sheltered existence and eventually repudiate her Republican roots and become a champion of Democratic causes. It should be noted that Hillary Clinton is extraordinarily smart. Her senior thesis advisor referred to her as the best student he had ever taught. She was a gifted student who took advantage of the many opportunities offered her during her four years at Wellesley. It is thus hardly surprising that she was accepted by both Harvard and Yale Law School. Hillary chose Yale Law School in part due to a chance meeting with a Harvard law professor who opined that women were not meant to be lawyers. Hillary claimed that she had already been leaning toward Yale's program, and the meeting with the curmudgeonly professor only cemented her decision to turn down Harvard's offer. This decision literally changed the path of her life, because it was at Yale that Hillary met her future husband, William Jefferson Clinton. The mythology of their meeting places them both at the library studying when Hillary finally walked up to Bill and said that if he was to keep on staring at her and she at him, he should at least know her name.[14]

Once they finally started dating, their relationship quickly became intense. According to many, Bill was able to bring out a more spontaneous Hillary. Hillary was no less serious at Yale than she was at Wellesley, or even in high school. As a law student, she was eminently successful, winning herself a position on the editorial board of the prestigious *Yale Law Journal*. Her position on the journal was no small achievement and was one signal to the political world that she was someone to take note of. Despite her commitment to academic and political endeavors, Bill managed to elicit from Hillary a bawdy sense of fun. Although the focus of this book is Hillary Clinton, it would be incomplete without providing some background on Bill Clinton. After all, he is one of the most famous public figures in the nation, if not the world, and his various escapades and achievements while governor and president figured prominently in Hillary Clinton's life and still influence how she is viewed by the public today.

Bill Clinton grew up in a small town in Arkansas and was raised by his mother, Virginia, after the death of his father before he was born. Trained as a nurse, Virginia Clinton had to support herself and her son on her own salary. In order to make more money, she trained as a nurse anesthetist and left her one-year-old son, Bill, with her mother and father.[15] She was gone for several years, and when she returned, Bill's grandmother was reluctant to give him up. After the death of his grandfather, he grew up largely surrounded by women, until his mother married Roger Clinton. Unfortunately, his stepfather was an abusive alcoholic, which forced Bill into an early adulthood. At the age of fourteen, Bill, already big for his age, stood up to his stepfather in order to make him stop abusing his mother.[16] According to Sheehy, much of Bill Clinton's childhood was spent deceiving the people around him. He never let on about the abuse taking place in his home or about his unhappiness. Instead, he listened to music, read books, and lived a life more in tune with the type of reality he found palatable.[17] Bill Clinton's intelligence took him away from Arkansas. After college, he was a Rhodes Scholar at Oxford and eventually attended Yale Law School, starting his first year during Hillary's second. Bill Clinton had a definite presence at Yale, although in his first year, he was often off campus more than on, working on the senate campaign of the liberal, antiwar candidate Joe Duffey. When on campus, Bill Clinton could often be heard extolling the virtues of his home state, telling his listeners of his plans to return to Arkansas to run for national office.[18]

Soon after Hillary made the first move and introduced herself, she and Bill Clinton began dating. Their first date demonstrated Bill's charisma. They were both interested in an exhibition at the campus museum. Upon finding it closed, Bill persuaded the janitor to open the museum for them if they picked up trash in exchange. Hillary was intrigued by his open approach with everyone. Bill Clinton's ability to talk to anyone and to improvise when faced with some obstacle (such as the inconvenience of museum operating hours), was very different from Hillary's more reserved approach to the world.[19] For all the questioning about their relationship, biographers and friends alike contend that for Hillary it was truly love at first sight. By the second year of their relationship, Bill and Hillary were sharing a house together. Bill Clinton managed to cut through Hillary's shyness and intensity, and they formed a relationship that endures today.

It did not hurt their relationship that Bill Clinton was an intellectual match for Hillary. Hillary was used to being the one who could almost always win a debate. This was not the case with Bill Clinton. While Hillary's intelligence stemmed from a quickness of understanding combined with studiousness and hard work, Bill seemed to be able to make connections across a variety of concepts and ideas. Despite the fact that he was frequently away from campus and missing classes, he would manage to catch up and still do well in his studies.

Hillary continued to be influenced by the times during which she attended law school. During her first year, Yale University became embroiled in a political rally supportive of the Black Panthers. While Hillary was still at Wellesley College, a former member of the Black Panthers, Alex Rackley, had been found dead in the Coginchaug River, which was about 25 miles north of New Haven. His corpse showed signs of torture (he had been shot, stabbed with an ice pick, burned with cigarettes and water, and even clubbed).[20] In the investigation, it was determined that Rackley was put on trial within the Black Panthers and executed for being a police informant. A witness ultimately claimed that it was Black Panther cofounder Bobby Seale who gave the order to kill Rackley.[21] Yale Law School students, who tended to be very liberal and socially active, quickly came to the defense of Seale and blamed the police for a flawed investigation. The students romanticized the Black Panthers as "urban Robin Hoods. Despite acting like thugs, and at times boasting of their thuggishness, they were given the benefit of the doubt and more, and the Panthers' argument that they were innocent victims of a police conspiracy was widely accepted."[22]

Seale was eventually indicted in August 1969, and the trial was held in New Haven. As a result, Yale University students held rallies in support of Seale. Hillary ended up volunteering for one of her professors, Thomas Emerson, to determine whether the Panthers who were on trial were having their civil rights abused. The trial gained so much attention that student protestors started arriving on the Yale University campus. Various groups called for students to strike, but ultimately the university president wisely canceled classes and allowed visits by the outside protestors. Not surprisingly, Hillary emerged from the general chaos of the time as one of the students able to negotiate between student demands and administration concerns. It probably did not hurt that she was already known on campus as a result of the *Life* article about her Wellesley College graduation speech. Again, one of the hallmarks of Hillary's approach was her desire to work within the existing institutional structures for keeping the lines of communication open between students and administration. While Hillary envisioned herself as someone who would be a political activist, she became more focused on working within the system, rather than from without.

Ultimately, though, Yale Law School served as the launching pad for what would become a lifelong passion of Hillary Clinton's: working to protect children. It was while she was at Yale that she met Marian Wright Edelman, founder of the Children's Defense Fund. During the summer after her first year at Yale, Hillary volunteered for Edelman's organization. Edelman initially discouraged her because there was no money available to pay for her time. However, Hillary obtained a grant to cover her costs, and she spent the summer working on Senator Walter Mondale's staff investigating the living condition of children of migrant workers. Based on this experience, she worked during her second year at the Yale Child Study Center, combining her legal studies with her newly found interest in children's issues. While at the center, Hillary focused on custody issues and ended up working with the New Haven Legal Services Association, learning more about family law. She had found her calling: protection of children within the existing legal structure. However, this future did not fall into place as immediately as she had anticipated—in part due to her relationship with Bill Clinton, but also due to several opportunities that were presented to her.

The activities surrounding the Black Panthers also played a role in Hillary Rodham's intellectual development. During the summer of 1971, after her second year of law school, she decided to gain experience in the law surrounding mass movements. She moved to Berkeley, California, to do an internship with Robert Treuhaft, who was one of the lawyers for the Black Panthers. While working for Treuhaft, Hillary also continued her interest in the poor and migrant laborers and worked on their behalf through advocacy and other volunteer activities. During her third year in law school, she and Bill Clinton moved in together and shared a small house in New Haven. Soon after, Hillary brought Bill home to Park Ridge to meet her family. The Rodhams found Bill sincere and personable but wondered what their daughter was doing with someone who spoke so emphatically about returning to Arkansas to work for political change there.[23] The summer following her third year, Bill and Hillary went to Texas to work on George McGovern's presidential campaign. She spent much of her time driving around Texas campaigning for McGovern. Little is known about the details of the Clintons' work for McGovern, except that they worked hard coordinating campaign efforts. However, the legacy of their work with McGovern has been that many political critics have used that summer in Texas to equate the Clintons with a more liberal outlook than they actually claim on many issues.

Although Hillary Rodham could have gone to work for numerous private law firms after her graduation, she chose to return to New Haven in 1972 for a fourth year while Bill Clinton finished up his studies. This allowed her to finish supplementing her law degree with the work at the Yale Child Study Center.[24] Her final achievement in her fourth year at Yale Law School was an article for the *Harvard Educational Review* on children's rights. In this piece, Hillary argued that children should not necessarily be considered legally incompetent, and that they can often make responsible decisions regarding their own future.[25] This piece has been used by many political opponents to claim that Hillary Clinton is an advocate for breaking up families and allowing children to sue their parents. In fact, the article says nothing of the sort. Nevertheless, upon concluding her studies, Hillary was clearly at an impasse about her future, both with regard to her career and her relationship with Bill Clinton. There are a multitude of sources indicating that even back in law school their relationship was tumultuous and that marriage was not automatically in the running. Indeed, the two fought often, and Hillary could not immediately decide what to do. Even though she took Bill home to meet her family, indicating a more serious relationship, she was wracked with indecision. In that first meeting with Hillary's family, Dorothy Rodham found Bill Clinton charming due to his eloquence, worldliness, and determination to return to the state he loved best. Her brothers formed a lifelong bond with Bill Clinton that resulted in their working on most of his election campaigns. Hugh Rodham thought enough about the young man his daughter brought home to stop Hillary's brother Hugh from exploiting Bill's good nature for help with yard work.[26] In retirement, the Rodhams would settle in Little Rock to be near the Clintons and their beloved granddaughter, Chelsea.[27]

In order to prepare herself for any eventuality, Hillary not only took the bar exam in Washington, D.C., but also went to Arkansas and sat for the state bar exam alongside Bill. Bill Clinton, in contrast, had no doubts about his future. He was intent, as he always said, to return to Arkansas to run for office. However, the options available for Hillary in Arkansas were not nearly as compelling as those available in Washington, D.C. Further complicating the issue was that Bill Clinton's ambitions for public office could be compromised by his relationship with Hillary. In a socially conservative state like Arkansas, love relationships that did not involve marriage could carry a stigma for political candidates.

Ultimately, the two went their different ways immediately upon graduation. Bill Clinton went to Fayetteville, Arkansas, to teach at the University of Arkansas Law School (and to gear up for his political run), and Hillary Rodham initially accepted a staff position at the Children's Defense Fund in Cambridge, Massachusetts. However, she would not be there for long. In January 1974, she moved to Washington, D.C., to work on the staff of John Doar, the special counsel for the impeachment hearings of President Nixon.[28] Hillary was given this opportunity through her connection to Yale Law School professor Burke Marshall, who worked with Doar. Hillary "played a prominent role from the beginning"[29] in Doar's staff. While most of the hired attorneys remained in the background (and indeed were known as the "faceless 40"),[30] Hillary often attended meetings with the Judiciary Committee members. She also worked with Bernie Nussbaum, who had been appointed by Doar to lead an independent investigation into Nixon's actions. Her most important role was to draft procedural rules for how the impeachment case would be presented to the House.[31] History records the results of the many hours of work put into investigating Nixon's actions. While three articles of impeachment were brought against Nixon (abuse of power, obstruction of justice, and contempt of Congress), Nixon resigned on August 9, 1974, before the impeachment hearings could begin. Many years later, Hillary Clinton would suffer the irony of having written the very same rules that were used against her own husband in the impeachment charges against President Clinton.

Upon Nixon's resignation, Hillary's Washington job was over. This relatively abrupt ending to a task on which she had spent many hours and months of her life provided her with a window of opportunity to determine the future direction of her life. While she was still unsure of the viability of her relationship with Bill Clinton, she knew that she wanted to pursue the possibility. The two kept in touch actively during their time apart, running up large phone bills. One weekend prior to the ending of the impeachment investigation, she made a trip down to Fayetteville to visit Bill. While there, she was offered a job teaching at the University of Arkansas Law School, which was trying to attract more accomplished attorneys to improve its national ranking. Upon the conclusion of her work for Doar, Hillary decided to do just that and moved to Arkansas to follow her heart and teach at the law school. Moving to Fayetteville was a big transition for a young woman who had always lived in more densely populated or urban settings. Although uncertain about whether it was the right choice, she felt that she needed to take the risk. And when she failed the Washington, D.C. bar exam but passed Arkansas's exam, she took that as a sign pointing her to a life with Bill.[32]

Hillary's decision to attend Yale Law School rather than Harvard shaped the course her life would take. She not only met her future husband as a result of that decision but also ended up forgoing a career as an extremely high-powered corporate lawyer, which she might otherwise have had. Although Hillary would work as a practicing attorney for many years while in Arkansas, it would not be the same caliber of work as the opportunities she might have taken outside Arkansas. However, the trade-off allowed her to fulfill her lifelong interest in civic engagement, which has ultimately resulted in her historic decision to run for president of the United States of America.

NOTES

1. Stephen J. Wayne, G. Calvin Mackenzie, and Richard L. Cole, *Conflict and Consensus in American Politics* (Belmont, Calif.: Thomson Wadsworth, 2007), p. 162.

2. Martha Sherrill, "The Rising Lawyer's Detour to Success," *The Washington Post*, January 12, 1993, p. B1.

3. Stephen J. Wayne, G. Calvin Mackenzie, and Richard L. Cole, *Conflict and Consensus in American Politics* (Belmont, Calif.: Thomson Wadsworth, 2007), p. 168.

4. Helen Kennedy, "60's Turmoil Turns Scholar into Rebel," *New York Daily News*, February 26, 2000, p. 26.

5. Martha Sherrill, "The Rising Lawyer's Detour to Success," *The Washington Post*, January 12, 1993, p. B1.

6. Ibid.

7. "Wellesley College 1969 Student Commencement Speech," Wellesley College Commencement Web site: http://www.wellesley.edu/PublicAffairs/Commencement/1969/053169hillary.html.

8. Gail Sheehy, *Hillary's Choice* (New York: Random House, 1999).

9. Hillary Rodham Clinton, *Living History* (New York: Simon and Schuster, 2003), p. 37.

10. "Reading Hillary Rodham's Hidden Thesis," MSNBC.com Web site: http://www.msnbc.msn.com/id/17388372/.

11. Ibid.

12. Martha Sherrill, "The Rising Lawyer's Detour to Success," *The Washington Post*, January 12, 1993, p. B1.

13. Gail Sheehy, *Hillary's Choice* (New York: Random House, 1999).

14. Hillary Rodham Clinton, *Living History* (New York: Simon and Schuster, 2003).

15. Gail Sheehy, *Hillary's Choice* (New York: Random House, 1999).

16. Ibid.

17. Ibid.

18. Hillary Rodham Clinton, *Living History* (New York: Simon and Schuster, 2003); Gail Sheehy, *Hillary's Choice* (New York: Random House, 1999); Joyce Milton, *The First Partner: Hillary Rodham Clinton* (New York: William Morrow and Company, 1999).

19. Joyce Milton, *The First Partner: Hillary Rodham Clinton* (New York: William Morrow and Company, 1999), p. 48.

20. Ibid., p. 35.

21. Ibid., p. 35.

22. Ibid., p. 35.

23. Martha Sherrill, "The Rising Lawyer's Detour to Success," *The Washington Post,* January 12, 1993, p. B1.

24. Joyce Milton, *The First Partner: Hillary Rodham Clinton* (New York: William Morrow and Company, 1999), p. 48.

25. Hillary Rodham, "Children Under the Law," *Harvard Educational Review* 43 (1973): 487–514.

26. Martha Sherrill, "The Rising Lawyer's Detour to Success," *The Washington Post,* January 12, 1993, p. B1.

27. Charles Babcock and Sharon LaFraniere, "The Clintons' Finances: A Reflection of Their State's Power Structure," *The Washington Post,* July 21, 1992, p. A7.

28. Joyce Milton, *The First Partner: Hillary Rodham Clinton* (New York: William Morrow and Company, 1999), p. 61.

29. Ibid., p. 63.

30. Ibid.

31. Ibid., p. 64.

32. Hillary Rodham Clinton, *Living History* (New York: Simon and Schuster, 2003).

Chapter 3

ARKANSAS

Not surprisingly, Hillary Rodham's life in Arkansas was substantially different from what she originally envisioned her life would be. She knew that if she were to have a future with Bill Clinton, it would be incumbent upon her to make the concessions necessary to make that happen; for as long as she had known him, it was clear that Bill Clinton intended to move back to Arkansas and run for public office. People who talk publicly about knowing Bill Clinton at Georgetown, Oxford, or Yale tell a similar story about him—that he was a young man in love with his home state and committed to a future that involved bettering that state. Thus, he was not going to remain on the East Coast despite the potential career opportunities available to both him and Hillary Rodham. Upon graduating from law school in 1973, Bill Clinton took a job teaching law at the University of Arkansas Law School in Fayetteville. He used his teaching position to establish himself in the state and begin a campaign for the U.S. Congress.

During a 1974 summer visit to Arkansas, Hillary Rodham found her boyfriend with his congressional race against Republican John Paul Hammerschmidt in full swing. Even her brothers went to Arkansas to help out on the campaign. This visit proved pivotal in the Clintons' relationship. While in Arkansas, the University of Arkansas Law School, trying to improve its national ranking, made it known that Hillary could have a position there if she wanted. With many promising career options in Washington, D.C., Hillary Rodham had a difficult decision to make. Should she pursue her career in the East or move for love to relatively small southern city in a fairly small and somewhat impoverished southern state? For the first time in her life, she chose love over her other ambi-tions.

A friend who helped her move from Washington to Fayetteville in 1974 remarked that despite deriding her for going to Fayetteville to "wind up married to some country lawyer,"[1] during the trip, she was cheerfully resolved to begin a new phase of her life. Other friends could not believe it when they heard that Hillary Rodham, rising legal star, would be mov-ing to Arkansas to teach in what was then a second-rate law school. Even her mother wondered if Arkansas would be good for her daughter but characteristically did not interfere with her daughter's decision. Her only explanation was that she loved Bill Clinton and had to go to see if the relationship could work out. Never before in her life had another human being had such a profound influence on the direction she took.[2] Hillary moved to Fayetteville and began teaching law school after her position with the Nixon impeachment committee came to an end upon Nixon's resignation. Her students in Arkansas were either barely younger than she or, more often the case, older. As a law professor, she was hardworking and competent, establishing the school's legal aid program. Meanwhile, Bill Clinton was traveling the state trying to beat a well-funded and fairly popular incumbent. While an uphill battle, he hoped that the anti-Nixon sentiment sweeping the country would benefit his candidacy. It was not to be. Bill Clinton lost his first campaign 52 percent to 48 percent. However, the following year, he finally persuaded Hillary Rodham to marry him. They were married on October 11, 1975.[3] The small wedding ceremony was held at the little house the young couple shared in Fayetteville. The bride wore a dress purchased with her mother the day before at a local department store. A reception was held by friends at their nearby home. Friends and family came from all over the country to help celebrate the special day.

As a young woman in Fayetteville, it was clear that Hillary Clinton was not sure about the path she would take. Clearly interested in public service, she tried to enlist in the Marine Corps, where she was turned away by the recruiter, who cited her age, poor vision, and gender.[4] There is some speculation that she was considering a position as an attorney in the armed services' Judge Advocate General (JAG) Corps. According to her White House spokesperson, "[s]he was exploring all her options, the National Guard, everything."[5]

While Bill Clinton lost his congressional campaign, he rebounded quickly and by 1976 was elected the attorney general for Arkansas. Un-like his congressional campaign, which was very competitive, the cam-paign for attorney general was uneventful. Having paid his dues to the

Arkansas Democratic Party and carrying his strong résumé of prestigious education and political activism, getting the nomination from the party was no problem for Bill Clinton. The Arkansas Republican Party could not even come up with an opponent. This relatively easy campaign provided the Clintons with time to work on behalf of Jimmy Carter's presidential campaign. Bill Clinton headed up the Arkansas effort, while Mrs. Clinton was sent to Indiana to be the field coordinator.[6]

In order to assume the attorney generalship, the Clintons needed to relocate from Fayetteville to Little Rock. As a result, Mrs. Clinton's career as law professor came to an end. She enjoyed teaching, but Fayetteville was too far away from Little Rock, where Bill Clinton needed to be for his new position. Due to potential for conflict of interest, Hillary decided that taking a position in state government or any other public job was in-advisable. She thus chose to become a member of a private law firm.[7] The Rose Law Firm became a household name as a result of her position in their offices and the scandals that would haunt Bill Clinton's presidential campaigns and Hillary Clinton's position as First Lady.

Hillary Clinton joined the litigation section of the law firm as the first female associate in the offices. She worked most closely with Vince Foster and Webster Hubbell (again, two names that were destined to become familiar to the entire nation). She was able to continue to pursue her interest in children's welfare through her law practice, and one of the first cases she tackled was to change the prohibition of foster parents from adopting their charges. As a result of this endeavor, she, along with others, formed the Arkansas Advocates for Children and Families, which continues to operate today. Hillary Clinton's position with the law firm not only enabled her to polish her considerable legal skills but also provided the Clintons with a comfortable income and allowed them to make greater inroads politically within the state. As a well-liked attorney general, Bill Clinton decided to throw his hat into the gubernatorial race in 1978 and won at the age of 32. In Arkansas, governors sit for only two-year terms.

In 1979, Mrs. Clinton was promoted to partner at Rose Law Firm, where she had a great deal of flexibility to pursue her long-standing commitment to public service. In her new position, she continued her work with the Children's Defense Fund and traveled regularly to Washington, D.C., for board meetings. As a result of working on his campaign, Hillary Clinton was also appointed by President Carter to the board of the Legal Services Corporation, which required Senate confirmation. The Legal Services Corporation was created by President Nixon and Congress to provide legal services to the poor. Given the First Lady's long history as an advocate for children and her position at the University of Arkansas

Law School, where she established the legal aid program, she was both well qualified and easily confirmed. In addition to her legal work and her work on corporate and nonprofit boards, Mrs. Clinton was also heading up the Rural Health Advisory Committee on behalf of her husband. It was during this period that the Clintons had their daughter, Chelsea, in 1980.[8]

While Hillary Clinton was clearly succeeding in her career, the Arkansas public was admittedly perplexed by their new First Lady. To begin, she decided to keep her maiden name rather than take her husband's last name or even hyphenate it with her own. Still a relatively unusual decision in the 1970s, it was particularly noteworthy in conservative Arkansas. Her intention to keep her maiden name was mentioned in the wedding announcement.[9] Perhaps even more bizarre to the locals was her insistence on ignoring her looks. She refused to do anything with her hair, did not wear makeup, and wore frumpy, unflattering clothes. The Clintons' longtime friend Linda Bloodworth-Thomason has remarked that "people thought she was a hippie."[10] Her failure to take more of an interest in her appearance is something that she has long been known for. In fact, her appearance continues to be noteworthy today. It is not unusual to see articles about her mode of dress, hairstyles, or figure. While all women in the public eye face scrutiny regarding their appearance, the attention that she has faced has been extensive. During the 1992 presidential campaign, Mrs. Clinton's past fashion sense, or lack thereof, was the subject of more than one newspaper article. There have been years of speculation and interest in her hairstyle, and indeed at one point while in the White House, there was a Web site dedicated to following her various styles. Her disregard for her physical appearance resulted in a tendency for the public to underestimate her, assuming she would be a quiet, devoted wife who would be supportive of her husband. They were not expecting someone as busy and actively engaged in her own career as she was. Arkansans were further surprised by the speed with which she returned to work after the birth of her daughter, Chelsea. Within six weeks, she was traveling again and leaving Chelsea at home with a close friend.

While the public may have been surprised by her behavior (or lack of interest in things considered more appropriate for a governor's wife), Bill Clinton himself was quickly losing the support with which he entered office. According to some, he assumed that his decisive victory (63%) translated into permission to make substantial changes to the state, a problem he would face when he took over the White House in 1993 as well. Unsurprisingly, he found support so long as he did not want to raise taxes or jeopardize long-standing benefits. Thus, when he decided to improve the highways and used an increase in licensing fees as the mechanism for financing, he immediately faced opposition. His solution only further angered the public.[11] Bill Clinton's approval ratings also suffered from taking too many Cuban refugees at the request of President Carter. As more and more refugees were arriving from Cuba on American soil, it was necessary to try to disperse them throughout the country. Some refugees came to the United States to escape Castro by sneaking out of the country, often on dangerous rafts, and crossing the ocean to Florida. Others came when Castro opened the prisons and allowed prisoners to seek political asylum in the United States rather than remain incarcerated. Ultimately, these two events combined made Bill Clinton an easy mark for his opponent during his first reelection campaign.

Although Bill Clinton decisively won his first gubernatorial election, he quickly found out the fickle ways of politics. At the time, he was seen as being out of touch with his fellow Arkansans, and in 1980, he lost his reelection bid and was out of a job. Mrs. Clinton, always a decisive and politically astute person, decided to take it upon herself to help in whatever way she could. While Bill Clinton graciously accepted teasing in political circles for going to Lamaze classes in 1979 and attending the birth of his daughter in 1980, it was clear to his wife that she needed to make some changes to allow her husband to better pursue his career objectives.[12] She finally decided to begin using her husband's last name when he opted to run for election once again in 1982. As a candidate's wife, Hillary Clinton also worked hard on her personal image. She started wearing soft contact lenses instead of her trademark thick glasses. She cut her hair, bought new clothes, made an effort to always leave the house wearing makeup, and even took to going to a hairstylist before special occasions.[13] The concern over her last name was only one superficial reminder of how much she sacrificed to marry Bill Clinton. She had been raised to pursue her own goals and graduated from a top law school with many options available to her. By moving to Arkansas, Mrs. Clinton in many ways decided to put her career second. While she did work full time and pursued numerous projects, she was always very aware of the impact of her actions on her husband's career. One could argue that it was not until 2000, when she decided to run for New York senator, that her own ambitions were finally placed front and center in her life. When asked in 1997 what he would do once he finished his second term as president, Bill Clinton would always remark that it would be a time for his wife to have a chance to pursue her career goals.

Bill Clinton was successful in his bid to regain the governor's mansion in 1982, and as first couple, the Clintons worked hard at a number of agendas they felt were important to the long-term success of their state.

Despite this commitment, Mrs. Clinton continued to work to support the family. As governor of Arkansas, Bill Clinton made a poor salary. Some of these efforts to support the family would later produce the fodder for the scandals that plagued the Clinton White House from the beginning. Interestingly, two of the scandals were a function of Mrs. Clinton's actions in Arkansas. The seriousness of the two actions—Whitewater and a small investment that resulted in a virtually unheard of level of return—depends on whether one believes Mrs. Clinton's explanations. For many people, that ultimately comes down to political affiliation. Supporters of the Clintons tended to be sympathetic to her justification and claim of a right-wing conspiracy out to get her and her husband, while those opposed to the Clintons found her explanations artful storytelling.

One of the first scandals pertained to an investment of $1,000 that Mrs. Clinton made in the commodities markets through a friend, Jim Blair, while in Arkansas. Hillary Clinton explained her decision to invest as a function of her need to make financial decisions for her family. In her memoir, she explains that her husband had very little interest in money—as long as he had enough to buy books and travel, he was content. However, she "worried that because politics is an inherently unstable profession, [they] needed to build up a nest egg."[14] When given the opportunity to invest in the commodities market with the advice of Blair, she jumped at the chance. The scandal component of this tale involved media reports that when she finally quit trading in the market, she had made a profit of $100,000—a 10,000 percent gain. This claim was not entirely true. Mrs. Clinton's investments were offset by losses as well. At the time she closed her account in 1980, the total profit was $72,996, a substantial gain from her initial investment, but not quite what the media originally claimed.[15] Hillary Clinton ended her foray into the commodities market when Chelsea was born because it proved too hard to manage with a new baby and a career. Many questioned the legitimacy of this success, which forced her to conduct a press conference while in the White House to help explain the outcome. This investment scandal never became the subject of a serious investigation because there was no real evidence of wrongdoing on the part of Mrs. Clinton.

Her investment in Whitewater Estates, however, was not so lucky. Indeed, this particular investment later became known as the Whitewater scandal and was thoroughly investigated throughout the bulk of Bill Clinton's presidency. The Whitewater investment was made with the Clintons' friends Jim and Susan McDougal. The Clintons and the McDougals purchased 230 acres of undeveloped land on the south bank of White River in North Arkansas.[16] Their intent was to develop the land

and then sell it at a profit. Interestingly, the Clintons did not have to put any money up for their portion of the investment; perhaps as a result, they failed to ask appropriate questions about the legitimacy of the McDougals' actions. The Clintons ended up being liable for the entire mortgage loan that was supposed to be shared with the McDougals.[17] The plan seemed to be a good one, but it ultimately fell victim to the rising interest rates of the times, and the land was never developed. The Clintons chose to listen to Jim McDougal's plans to avoid foreclosure on their loan rather than pay it off, which lead them into the scandal that pursued them throughout Bill Clinton's presidency.

One of Governor Clinton's goals after winning in 1982 was to focus on education in Arkansas. Focusing on the need to succeed in this effort, Bill Clinton made a decision that would be replicated once he took office as president: having his wife chair a commission, in this case to reform education for Arkansas. Although Mrs. Clinton thought it was a risky move, Bill Clinton was insistent that it would signal the seriousness with which he took the need to improve education in his home state. Education reform was not an easy task and faced considerable opposition from many groups, particularly teachers, who disliked the idea of mandatory teacher testing. Persuaded to take on the role created by her husband, Hillary Clinton pursued her quest for education reform the way that she pursued most goals. She methodically went from county to county and held hearings in each one to gather firsthand information regarding the state of education across Arkansas. Her county-by-county tour was very successful in terms of its policy goals, but it also played an important role in the Clintons' political success. People across the state, power brokers and everyday citizens alike, got to know and respect the First Lady for her considerable intellectual abilities, commitment to public service, and general competence. Mrs. Clinton greatly endeared herself to the people of the state, despite the controversial nature of the topic as well as the proposed reforms.[18]

Hillary Clinton by this point had completed her fairly drastic makeover. She eschewed her beloved granny dresses in favor of more stylish clothing and also styled her hair in a more flattering fashion. She even acquired a southern accent that she put to good use in appropriate settings. Her softer accent was appreciated by the power elite of the state. Not only had she become Mrs. Bill Clinton, instead of Hillary Rodham, but she had started dressing the part, complete with Easter hats.[19] Her outward transformation assisted her with her efforts to reform the state's educational system. By the time that she testified before the state legislature on the proposed education reforms, she had won over her most ardent detractors—one even went so far as to say that the wrong Clinton had been elected.[20] Her attention to looking the way that Arkansans expected a First Lady to look lent her a legitimacy that she had trouble capturing in the past. Changing education in Arkansas was one of the hallmarks of Governor Clinton's administration and was even hailed by the Reagan administration as one of the most successful state improvements. Bill Clinton's decision to put his wife in charge of the effort paid off; unfortunately, this success would not replicate itself in the future with national health care policy.

Bill Clinton's governorship ran fairly smoothly the second time around. While Mrs. Clinton was very involved in all aspects of her husband's political career, she was also able to pursue a few of her own goals in addition to educational reform. In this period, she was appointed to the Wal-Mart and TCBY boards of directors and was instrumental in helping Wal-Mart become environmentally friendly with a recycling program.[21] During her career in Arkansas, Hillary Clinton was twice named one of the 100 most influential attorneys in the United States.[22]

Bill Clinton served as governor of Arkansas until he ran for president in 1992. His strong reelection margin in 1986 was a clear indication of not only his popularity with the citizenry but also his general success at statewide politics. He successfully lobbied the state legislature to change the length of the governor's term from two to four years. This provided him with more security than he enjoyed previously. It also allowed him to decide whether to make a run for president. He had already been named the chairman of the National Governors Association, which assured him national recognition and status as an assumed player in presidential politics. In 1985, Bill Clinton became one of the founding members of the Democratic Leadership Conference (DLC), an organization aimed at moving the Democratic Party more toward the ideological middle in order to more easily win national and statewide elections.[23]

In 1988, the Democratic Party was wide open regarding potential candidates running for the nomination. The assumed nominee, Gary Hart, quickly self-destructed when he challenged the media to find evidence of extramarital affairs. The press had little trouble doing so, and Hart had to put an end to his presidential aspirations. Despite the seemingly open field, Bill Clinton simply could not decide whether it was his time to run or not. According to some sources, Hillary Clinton was strongly in favor of his running and was mobilizing effort to support his cause;[24] she was bitterly disappointed when he chose not to run for president. Explanations for this decision vary from speculation about vulnerability caused by extramarital affairs to the Clintons' contention that the timing was not right because of the impact a campaign would have had on Chelsea.[25]

Mrs. Clinton explained that right before making his final decision, Bill was asked by Chelsea where they would be going for vacation that year. When he responded that he might be unable to go on a vacation because of campaigning for president, Chelsea replied that she and her mother would go on their own. According to Bill Clinton, he then realized that he was not ready to make a run and sacrifice his time with his daughter.[26] Other biographies suggest that Chelsea served as a face-saving explanation and that the real reason that Bill Clinton opted out of the campaign that everyone assumed was going to happen (even several of his closest friends flew into Little Rock in order to be on hand for his presumed declaration into the presidential race) was the liability of his philandering past. Seeing that Gary Hart's past career had been ruined by his extramarital affair, Bill Clinton worried about the role his own past could play with regard to his political ambitions. While Bill Clinton did not end up running that time around, he did make his first big national television appearance in 1988 as the person chosen to introduce Michael Dukakis as the Democratic presidential nominee. The speech went on for so long that delegates to the convention cheered when Bill Clinton spoke the words "in conclusion."[27]

While much is made of the nature of the relationship between Bill and Hillary Clinton, there is little doubt that they have forged a symbiotic partnership where the strengths of one covers for the weaknesses of the other. While Mrs. Clinton was raised with the express intention of forging her own career and identity, she ultimately sacrificed a considerable amount of her individual ambition in order to secure the future of her husband. When she worked by his side, his career tended to flourish; when she pulled away, he floundered.[28] At least one friend remarked that while it was clear that the Clintons did not have the perfect relationship, it was well accepted that they were a powerful team with a strong bond holding them together.[29] The period immediately following Bill Clinton's decision not to run for president was one such time when Mrs. Clinton appeared to pull back from her husband, both politically and personally. There is speculation in some biographies of Hillary Clinton that during this time she was thinking very seriously about divorcing her husband. However, by 1990, it appeared that she decided to remain with him and continue to pursue their joint goal of a Clinton presidency,[30] which would happen in 1992.

In 1990, Bill Clinton faced, for the second time, a serious Republican challenge to the governor's office. Former Democrat Sheffield Nelson ran a dirty negative campaign, rife with rumors of corruption and marital infidelity. While the eventual election margin showed Governor Clinton

Chapter 4

THE 1992 CAMPAIGN

While Hillary Clinton's education about the life of an elected political family began in Arkansas, the 1992 presidential campaign of her husband completed the process. As a gubernatorial candidate's wife in Arkansas, Hillary Clinton discovered that she was occasionally out of step with many Arkansans, particularly regarding her initial decision not to take her husband's last name. As a presidential candidate's wife, she subsequently learned that almost anything she did during Bill Clinton's presidential campaign was bound to offend one group or another and that she would be scrutinized and criticized time and again. From the time Bill Clinton first ran for president until today, Mrs. Clinton's role as wife has been nontraditional and constantly open to scrutiny.

In order to win the presidency, a candidate must first win nomination from a political party with a guaranteed spot on the ballot or must launch a successful alternative candidacy that involves getting a place on the ballot in the 50 states. Bill Clinton, a longtime party loyalist, sought the Democratic nomination in 1992. Ideologically, both Clintons tended toward moderation. Hillary Rodham Clinton always functioned under the assumption that working within the system to create change was the best alternative. Bill Clinton functioned the same way but was also more personally centrist. Neither of the Clintons was so polarized to the left of the ideological spectrum that they felt compromise with voices on the right impossible. During the 1980s, Bill Clinton, first as a member and later as president of the Democratic Leadership Council (DLC), aligned himself with other centrist Democrats who felt that the way to keep and win the national office was through a set of moderate policies that would benefit average Americans. As political leaders in Arkansas, both Clintons seemed to take a rather academic approach to democracy and recognized both the power of finding a middle ground as well as the power of drawing in public support for a centrist set of ideas. In keeping with this philosophy, the Clintons began the 1992 campaign for the Democratic presidential nomination with the idea that they could successfully win a war of ideas as long as they could keep their centrist policy ideas at the forefront of the political debate.

Initially, the 1992 Democratic field was replete with candidates. The main competition that Bill Clinton faced was from three sitting senators, Bob Kerrey (NE), Tom Harkin (IA), and Paul Tsongas (MA).[1] The incumbent president seeking reelection was Republican George Bush. Bush had competition for the right wing of the party from Patrick Buchanan, former Nixon speechwriter turned television journalist.[2] Both parties faced competition from billionaire Ross Perot, who was using his personal fortune to wage a third-party attempt to seize the presidency.

In the two-party nominating system, the first and most important events of the nominating season are the Iowa caucuses and the New Hampshire primary. Winners of these events prove that they have staying power, look more legitimate to voters in the rest of the country, and gather what political scientists refer to as political momentum. Political momentum during the presidential nominating season refers to the progressive collection of more campaign donations, more public legitimacy, and subsequently more delegates to the national convention and begins with strong showings in early races. The Clintons spent a great deal of time in New Hampshire, correctly assuming that the Iowa caucuses, the first event in the nominating season, would easily be won by Senator Harkin. Bill Clinton took a strong second place in New Hampshire to Tsongas, in part because the Clintons spent countless hours reaching out to voters on an individual basis. The New Hampshire results were crucial. As a fiscally conservative Democrat and a New Englander, Tsongas was the overwhelming favorite in New Hampshire. However, Bill Clinton's charm, well-directed campaign, and moderate message made him particularly well favored by New Hampshire voters who had seen him in person. When Tsongas dropped out of the race in March 1992, all the speculation turned to the candidate with the next largest number of delegates, Bill Clinton. There was much speculation in the press at the time over whether Bill Clinton could win the general election. That speculation only increased when, by April, it was clear that Bill Clinton had the nomination. The Clintons worked tirelessly to make sure that they, as a couple, presented the image necessary to win.

One of the biggest challenges facing the Clintons during the election was the ongoing speculation about their marriage and the behavior of Bill Clinton with other women. Whereas such speculation might have occurred—and indeed, according to some, Bill Clinton's infidelities kept him out of the 1988 campaign—for the most part, the Arkansas media rarely published any stories about his private life.[3] While many people knew about Bill Clinton's alleged affairs while he was attorney general and governor,[4] it wasn't considered relevant for the public domain in Arkansas. That was simply not the case in the presidential election. This can be explained by several changing factors:

1. The tradition before the Vietnam War and Watergate was for the media to treat a candidate's private life as sacrosanct. However, after those two events, the media and the public felt betrayed by governmental officials lying to them, which created an even more antagonistic relationship between the media and public officials.

2. The mechanisms of news delivery changed in the period between Watergate and the 1992 presidential election. The advent of 24-hour cable news networks like CNN meant that there was more time to fill, so the cable networks were looking for more stories. In addition, reporting itself was changing. News was becoming a form of entertainment, and in order to keep viewers, readers, and/or listeners, media outlets deemed it necessary to provide their audiences with more of the kinds of stories that would keep them tuned in. This meant more stories about the personal lives of candidates.

3. The rising popularity of AM talk radio provided ideologically leaning broadcasters with a venue for their particular soapboxes, which often included personal scrutiny of candidates who were not favored. Since the news media comprise competitive and profit-driven businesses, even the more traditional media outlets like newspapers and network news altered their traditions to include candidates' personal peccadilloes as part of normal coverage.

4. A shrinking zone of privacy became the tradition after the 1988 election.[5] The Clintons suffered somewhat from the effects of Gary Hart's hubris. When Hart famously challenged the media to find evidence of extramarital affairs, all television crews needed to do was follow him to a liaison with his girlfriend and then broadcast the videotape on national television. In so

doing, the genie came out of the bottle, and future candidates would find that their zone of privacy was ever shrinking.

One could also argue that, to some degree, Bill Clinton brought the speculation about his private life on himself by inviting the public into his private life; he tended to answer any number of questions that were deeply personal and not terribly relevant to his candidacy, such as whether he wore boxers or briefs. By answering the question Bill Clinton legitimized being asked such personal questions and blurred the lines between what is personal and what is public. He also tried to present himself as a regular guy whom people would want to "have a beer with." So, he often appealed to his humble roots and personal life experiences, and he engaged the growing infotainment industry by appearing in venues like Oprah Winfrey's show and Arsenio Hall's late-night television show, during which he famously played the saxophone. While this affability may have invited speculation into the Clintons' personal life, it also helped Bill Clinton win the presidency in 1992. As an accessible and likable person, he provided a strong contrast to the sitting president. When President Bush appeared on MTV, he appeared stiff and uncomfortable. When he tried to stage press events in public places, he seemed out of touch. The most famous example was a stop in a supermarket, where the president remarked at great length about "cool" scanner technology at the checkout. His exuberance backfired because the technology had been in place for years, and it made him seem out of touch with everyday people.[6]

Early in the 1992 nomination campaign, Gennifer Flowers held a press conference to tell her story of a long-term romantic relationship with the candidate, Bill Clinton. Gennifer Flowers was a longtime lounge singer and former state employee who told a dramatic tale of love and sexual addiction, complete with audiotapes that were supposed to be the governor leaving messages on her answering machine.[7] While the story began in the tabloid media, it quickly jumped to more respectable venues and took the oxygen out of the other issues in the campaign. While the candidate and his surrogates wanted to talk politics and public policy, the only questions being asked were about Gennifer Flowers. Bill Clinton's instinct was to ignore the story and continue on as before. Hillary Clinton's instinct was to take on the issue and fight back. She eventually got her way as the mainstream media picked up the tabloid story. The Clintons appeared on *60 Minutes* following the Super Bowl, which provided tremendous viewership, where they were asked about the state of their relationship. Before the interview, it is reported that Mrs. Clinton was afraid that she would cry.[8] However, she was stalwart, looking intently at her husband as he spoke, sometimes with her arm around his waist. During this interview, Bill Clinton admitted to causing pain in his marriage but stated that the marriage was strong, that both he and his wife constantly worked on making it stronger. He thus implicitly admitted to his infidelities, or at least to the one. In a quote reprinted and rebroadcast across the nation, Mrs. Clinton famously said in her adopted southern accent, "I'm not sittin' here, some little woman, standin' by my man like Tammy Wynette.... I'm sittin' here because I love him and I honor what he's been through and what we've been through together, and, you know, if that's not enough for people, then heck, don't vote for him."[9] After a formal public complaint from Tammy Wynette, Mrs. Clinton apologized for disparaging the singer.

In addition, Mrs. Clinton went on the offensive in other media venues. In a feature article about her in the May 1992 issue of *Vanity Fair* magazine, the candidate's wife said that she did not know what the big deal was about her husband when George Bush was well known to have had affairs. She later apologized publicly to the Bushes, saying, "It was a mistake.... People were asking me questions at the time and I responded, but nobody knows better than I the pain that can be caused by ever discussing rumors in private conversation."[10] Mrs. Clinton's apology was very telling. She apologized for bringing up an emotionally difficult subject but never denied her accusation. Many political analysts credit Mrs. Clinton with effectively quashing much of the public speculation about her husband's affairs by sending a signal to the Bush campaign that if their personal life was open for examination, so was the president's. Her defense of her husband's campaign helped give her a reputation as ruthless and cold, while freeing the candidate to be affable, good-natured, and accessible.

The Clinton campaign also went to great lengths to discredit Flowers's tapes. The audio quality was poor, and the argument was made that the tapes were doctored. Since Flowers was also clearly enjoying the media attention, questions were raised about whether she made up the story to get attention or whether a political opponent had compensated her for coming forward. As is now public knowledge, Gennifer Flowers was not the only relationship that Bill Clinton had outside of his marriage, though probably few people know just how many affairs he has had. In any case, by appearing on *60 Minutes* with his wife by his side and appearing to answer the question about his affair(s), Bill Clinton saved his campaign and came in second in the New Hampshire primary. He was then dubbed the comeback kid, both for overcoming his disastrous introduction of Michael Dukakis in 1988 and for his ability to garner votes in the wake of a personal scandal.

The Clintons were bolstered during this emotional ordeal by countless friends and family members who rallied around them. Some even went to work on the campaign in order to make sure that no such slipups happened again. One of Hillary Clinton's closest friends, Susan Thomases, became Bill Clinton's scheduler. Another friend, Brooker Shearer, spent nine months of 1992 on the road with Hillary Clinton. Television producer Linda Bloodworth-Thomason described the motivation as akin to enlisting to fight in a just war.[11]

The Clintons made it clear to the U.S. public that they were something of a package deal. Never before had the nation seen a potential First Lady who was an accomplished career woman and policy advocate in her own right. This new role raised the consternation of both the public and the media. Mrs. Clinton often came under intense scrutiny for her words and actions. She and her husband quickly discovered that the media have a tendency to take a quote out of context, which can lead to trouble. At one campaign stop, Bill Clinton, highlighting his wife's expertise on children's issues, suggested that electing him would benefit voters because the public would be getting two for the price of one.[12] Hillary Clinton's campaign staff also adopted the slogan "buy one, get one free," which ultimately led to criticism that she was overreaching her position and would have undue influence on the president. This scrutiny by the news outlets then bled into the infotainment media as well, and talk show hosts started to ask questions about who really wore the pants in the Clintons' relationship. Entertainers developed a set of jokes critical of Mrs. Clinton, which plagued her for the eight years Bill Clinton served as president.

It was not just the behavior of Mrs. Clinton that brought greater scrutiny about her potential role as First Lady, it was also the contrast between her and the other two major candidates' wives, Barbara Bush and Margot Perot. Mrs. Bush tended to publicly play the more traditional role of First Lady. While Mrs. Bush willingly went out on the campaign trail for her husband, it was clear that she was not interested in having any formal policy role, and the Bush family was never candid about the role she played with the president. In the case of Margot Perot, she was almost never even seen on the campaign trail. The Perot campaign was very much focused on the candidate and his particular political agenda. Perhaps like the wives of many successful businessmen, Mrs. Perot was satisfied with a low-key role.

Hillary Clinton in many ways set herself up for intense scrutiny by establishing her own staff to assist her in her husband's campaign. This defied standard protocol, in which the presidential candidate's staff controlled all of the surrogates' scheduling and messages, including those of the candidate's wife. However, she was a different sort of wife who was very involved in all of her husband's campaigns; the presidential campaign would be no different.

Scrutiny of the Clintons' relationship also meant scrutiny of the role that Mrs. Clinton would play if she were to take office. This nation had never really known a politically active First Lady. The closest was Eleanor Roosevelt, who made an effort to raise public awareness of certain issues and was very much criticized in the press for her behavior. While Roosevelt held a formal position as assistant director of the Office of Civilian Defense for five months, she was not charged with making policy. The same was true for Rosalynn Carter's appointment as honorary chair of the President's Commission on Mental Health. This is a nation very rooted in its beliefs about gender roles, and many opponents successfully played on fears that a professional First Lady involved in the government would be somehow bad for the nation. The foundation for those fears stemmed from Hillary Clinton's own reputation within the political arena, separate from that of her husband. While the general public may not have been aware of who she was, by virtue of her résumé, they quickly came to realize that Hillary Clinton would not be the traditional First Lady in the mold of Barbara Bush or Nancy Reagan. While all First Ladies tend to pursue their own goals, the traditional expectation is that they do so outside of the legislative arena and are not generally interested in making public policy. Mrs. Bush's commitment to literacy is an example. She used her role as First Lady to raise awareness of illiteracy nationwide and to remove the stigma and encourage the illiterate to seek services to get literate. Hillary Clinton, in contrast, assumed that she would be an active part of her husband's administration. She had done so while he was governor of Arkansas, so the assumption was that she would continue to do so from the White House. However, many voters and political analysts were uncomfortable with that kind of relationship and unsure of what it would mean for the nation.

An ongoing theme for Mrs. Clinton was her constant suppression of her own self-ambition in order to ensure the success of her husband. Perhaps nowhere was this suppression seen so clearly as when Bill Clinton ran for office in 1992. It became readily apparent that Hillary Clinton was a lightning rod for much of the public who were not comfortable with such an activist wife. She did not help her own cause when she made a comment about choices women make in terms of whether she should have stayed home to bake cookies. Though the comment was not intended to denigrate stay-at-home moms, taken out of context, it clearly did. Hillary Clinton had to learn one of the critical lessons of any campaign: staying on message. It became paramount for her to not say anything off script. Moreover, as she made appearances as one of the surrogates for her husband, she had to be sure to minimize her own role, despite her initial assumptions that she would be playing a strong role in her husband's administration.

If all of these challenges were not enough for Mrs. Clinton, there was the ongoing battle over her appearance. While she was ridiculed to some extent by Arkansans about her appearance, particularly her apparent lack of interest in how she looked, she fared little better in the national spotlight, despite having made changes for her public life in Arkansas. This is the stage when Hillary Clinton was mocked for constantly changing her hairstyle. While she claimed that it was fun to suddenly be given makeovers, the media constantly pointed out how her appearance kept changing.[13] Her headband was no longer acceptable, and she had to go through various metamorphoses to find a style that would suit her. Discussion about her looks, clothing, and words made it very clear that running for a presidential election was a very different task than running in a small, southern state gubernatorial election. Perhaps as a consequence of the focus on things that Mrs. Clinton did not find so important, her relationship with the media was always fraught with tension at best and hostility at worst. Of course, one of the other reasons that she tended to distrust the media was their unwelcome (in her mind) focus on Bill Clinton's extramarital relationships. She did not find it appropriate that they should dwell on such issues, which created a chilly interaction with the media. There would never be a time while she was living in the White House that the First Lady would not feel slightly antagonistic toward the media. Unfortunately, this antagonism led to poor decisions when facing various scandals during the Clinton presidency. If she had had a better relationship with the media, perhaps she would not have resorted to a bunker mentality when questions arose about her involvement in various situations, such as Whitewater. Since Mrs. Clinton never trusted the media to fairly represent her, her natural instinct was to withhold information, which only served to intensify the difficult relationship with the media. She answered questions when asked but rarely volunteered information.

Bill Clinton's choice of a running mate, Al Gore, was an attempt to bring a kind of traditional seriousness to the campaign as well as solidify the ticket's appeal to southern voters. Gore, the senator from Tennessee, son of a senator, and Vietnam veteran, was smart and also interested in long-term policy debates as well as a centrist approach to policy. Gore also brought to the ticket a more traditional political wife. Tipper Gore used her role as a senator's wife to advocate for warning labels on music and music videos to protect children. The Clintons and the Gores quickly forged a strong political foursome, and the two wives often made campaign appearances together. Images of either the two candidates with their wives, on their own, or together sent a message of youth and vitality to U.S. voters, and the polls subsequently reflected this positive image.

The Clintons' lives took a great deal of scrutiny during the campaign. Speakers at the Republican National Convention did their best to present Mrs. Clinton as a radical feminist who likened marriage to slavery and who wanted to destroy the American family. Candidate Bill Clinton was portrayed as a womanizing, draft-dodging upstart overly dominated by his wife. However, the Clintons were undaunted in the wake of these attacks. They responded to every shot, working hard to keep smiles on their faces and to keep the discussion focused on a common set of policy issues. The Clintons depended on a few trusty advisors to make sure they stayed on message. James Carville, the political director for the campaign, famously placed a set of reminders near his desk that were used as a mantra:

Change vs. more of the same
The economy, stupid
Don't forget health care[14]

Examine the transcripts of speeches and press conferences, and it is clear that the candidate, Mrs. Clinton, and the Gores stayed on point, delivered the message, and worked diligently to keep the campaign focused on policy issues.

Despite the positive components of the campaign, Mrs. Clinton's role as wife came under constant scrutiny, and when she seemed to step beyond the limits of that role, she came under fire. She struggled to find her own voice, but one that would not hurt her husband. This was a struggle that she fought for the entire time that Bill Clinton was in office. During his administration, her role would evolve from being an active policy maker as head of the task force to change health care to that of the wife standing by her husband. It was never an easy balancing act for her to maintain, and, arguably, only after Bill Clinton left the White House was she able to finally realize her own ambitions without the need for reining in her intelligence and interest in activism.

So what kind of impact did Hillary Clinton actually have on her husband's election? Clearly, he succeeded, and she was influential in creating that victory. Mrs. Clinton was a big part of all her husband's campaigns, lending advice and forging strategy. Despite an undercurrent of criticism in the press, Mrs. Clinton remained a stalwart campaigner and even resigned herself to many of the more traditional roles assumed by candidates' wives. Were it not for her actions, allegations of marital infidelity may well have torpedoed Bill Clinton's quest for the presidency. During the final stretch of the presidential campaign, the Clintons and the Gores took to the road in buses to make stops all over the country.

One of the keys to the success of the bus tour was the portrayal of both the Clintons and the Gores as accessible, bright, and young. The tour was specifically designed to present both Clintons as the antithesis of the incumbent Bushes, who were depicted as conservative, old, and out of touch with everyday reality. President Bush played into the hands of these depictions on a few occasions that did nothing to improve his image in the public's eye. At each so-called bus stop, the campaigning first couple and their running mates would emerge bright eyed, cheerful, and ready to talk policy. Both Clintons were articulate and adept at such discussions, and few could counter the would-be president's enthusiasm for talking policy.

In the end, Bill Clinton won the election by a plurality, 43 percent of the vote. Bush received 38 percent, and Perot, who dropped out of the race in the summer only to reenter in the fall with a strange explanation about the persecution of his family, received 19 percent. The country clearly favored Bill Clinton, and the voting results showed that a strong political wife could mean victory. Unfortunately for the Clintons, their first two years in the White House were plagued by miscalculations over what they thought the U.S. citizenry would be willing to accept in terms of a formal role for the First Lady.

NOTES

1. There were some other candidates in the race: Douglas Wilder of Virginia and Jerry Brown of California were contenders but never serious competition to Bill Clinton or any of the other potential frontrunners. Brown stayed in the race for several months but never amassed many delegates.

2. The president's competition from Buchanan meant that he had to speak more carefully to the conservative base of the Republican Party. This meant, among other things, that the fairly centrist Republican had to take more vocal and strident policy stands on issues like abortion, issues that he might have normally ignored or simply given lip service to in order to keep the conservative base happy.

3. The official story from the Clintons is that he chose not to run because daughter Chelsea was too young.

4. Gail Sheehy, *Hillary's Choice* (New York: Random House, 1999).

5. Doris Graber, *Mass Media and American Politics*, 7th ed. (Washington, D.C.: CQ Press, 2006).

6. In reality, as vice president or president for the previous 12 years, Mr. Bush was in the White House when the technology appeared in grocery stores. It is not reasonable to expect that the vice president or the president would spend time in grocery stores. The logistics for the Secret Service alone would make such outings impractical.

7. Elizabeth Drew, *On the Edge: The Clinton Presidency* (New York: Simon and Schuster, 1995).

8. Martha Sherrill, "The Education of Hillary Clinton," *The Washington Post,* January 13, 1993, p. D1.

9. Ibid.

10. Deborah Sontag, "The 1992 Campaign: Candidate's Wife; Hillary Clinton: Speaking About Rumors," *New York Times*, April 5, 1992, p. A22.

11. Ibid.

12. Hillary Rodham Clinton, *Living History* (New York: Simon and Schuster, 2003).

13. Ibid.

14. Charles O. Jones, "Campaigning to Govern: The Clinton Style," in *The Clinton Presidency,* ed. Colin Campbell and Bert A. Rockman (Chatham, N.J.: Chatham House Publishers, 1996), pp. 15–50.

Hillary Rodham at Wellesley. Getty Images.

October 11, 1975: Bill and Hillary Clinton on their wedding day. William J. Clinton Presidential Library.

*March 4, 1980: Little Rock,
Arkansas: Bill and Hillary on the day
they brought newly born Chelsea V.
Clinton home from the hospital.
William J. Clinton Presidential
Library.*

*President Clinton dances with
Mrs. Clinton at one of the
inaugural balls, January 20,
1993. William J. Clinton Presidential Library.*

President and Mrs. Clinton at Chelsea's Sidwell Friends School graduation ceremony, 1997. William J. Clinton Presidential Library.

Hillary Rodham Clinton participates in a photo shoot for Ladies Home Journal, March 2000. William J. Clinton Presidential Library.

Senator Clinton speaks at a campaign rally in Keene, New Hampshire (July 2007) with former President Bill Clinton in the background. Jodi Hilton/ The New York Times/Redux.

President Clinton and Hillary Rodham Clinton pose for their annual Christmas portrait, December 3, 2000. William J. Clinton Presidential Library.

Senator Clinton on tour in Jerusalem (November 2005). Rina Castelnuovo/The New York Times/Redux.

Chapter 5

THE FIRST TERM

When Bill and Hillary Clinton moved into the White House, it was with the idealistic expectation that their ideas had won them the election and that they would be able to begin implementation of those ideas right away. In keeping with their long time way of doing business, the Clintons expected to have a policy-oriented partnership to complement their personal partnership. When it came time to develop the president's cabinet and to choose White House staff, a small group of trusted advisors sat down with the president-elect in Little Rock, Arkansas. One of the people at the table most of the time was Mrs. Clinton.[1] The group knew that they had to be very careful with their choices because they had big plans in the policy arena.

It had been 12 years since a Democrat held the White House, and so key people from Carter's administration were aging. In addition, since President Carter had lost his bid for a second term, the selection group generally tended to view people who had served under him as unacceptable candidates unless they had gone on to distinguish themselves since 1980. There was also a preference amongst the decision makers for choosing youth and idealism over Washington experience for a number of reasons. They were young and idealistic themselves, and with the exception of the vice president–elect (also an idealist), they were largely people who were accomplished outside the Beltway. The end result was a cabinet and staff that had little Washington policy experience. This lack of experience in the White House would come back to haunt the Clintons before the end of their first year in office.[2]

The planning process included Mrs. Clinton having her own West Wing office and West Wing staff in addition to the more traditional East Wing office and staff. The group considered having Mrs. Clinton assume the position of domestic policy advisor, but it was determined that she could essentially have the role without the title, which would be less threatening to the public.[3] The decision over the West Wing offices was fairly controversial among the group in Little Rock that was planning the transition and the cabinet. At least one advisor, Vernon Jordan, is reported to have opposed the move, arguing that it would be too hard for the U.S. public to understand, and feared that the current of resistance to Mrs. Clinton seen during the campaign would quickly rise again.[4] Until 1993, a First Lady had never had an office in the West Wing, or a staff to go along with it. Mrs. Clinton's chief of staff, Margaret Williams, was also to serve as an assistant to the president, a dual role never before seen in the White House. The Williams appointment meant that there would be a direct chain of communication between the president and the First Lady's staff on policy issues. More than one analysis of the presidency has called Mrs. Clinton the president's key advisor.[5] There is even some documentation that cabinet members like Donna Shalala, secretary of Health and Human Services, and Carol Rosco, chief domestic policy advisor, reported to Mrs. Clinton on at least some issues early on.[6]

While there are some real criticisms to be made of Mrs. Clinton's ideas regarding White House procedures and staffing, not all of her ideas with regard to transition were controversial or even failures. One idea that she was successfully able to bring to fruition was the idea of having a campaign style war room set up to deal with policy initiatives that were particularly important to the president. This organizational structure was intended to make sure that they were able to keep control of the spin on the policy question at hand. As in the campaign, the idea was to make sure that "no charges went unanswered within the same news cycle."[7] The war room approach worked well in a number of policy campaigns but could not help the coveted health care plan because of delays in bringing out the plan as well as obstructions from Congress in terms of re-creating the idea as legislation.

In many ways, the Clinton White House was shaping up to be different from past administrations. The plan early on was also to give the vice president, Al Gore, a bigger role than had previously been played by vice presidents. This new role for the vice president grew out of the real admiration and appreciation that the president-elect developed for his running mate. However, even the vice president had fewer senior-grade assistants than the First Lady, a key sign of her relative power in the new

White House.[8] At the beginning of the first term, Mrs. Clinton was a key speaker at a major Camp David retreat in January intending to chart out the policy path that the new administration would take.[9] Reports indicate that Mrs. Clinton spelled out the ambitious domestic policy plan for the administration to pursue by arguing that if they were not going to go for the whole agenda in the first year, then they had failed the mission of the campaign.[10] Her role at Camp David and in other policy-planning areas has caused some analysts of the Clinton administration to charge that Mrs. Clinton was acting more like the chief of staff than the First Lady.[11]

The stark contrast between Mrs. Clinton and Mrs. Bush, the First Lady from 1988 to 1992, led to research by political scientists to formally study First Ladies, their roles, and public response to them.[12] While it has long been standard procedure to send first wives out as surrogates for their husbands, Hillary Clinton clearly went beyond what most had done before her. Tien, Checchio, and Miller[13] identify three different roles that First Ladies have played. The first, hostess, is the most traditional approach to the position. Typical activities for these women include those that are more ceremonial in nature, such as Nancy Reagan's raising money to refurnish the White House.[14] While Mrs. Clinton played hostess for her husband when he was governor of Arkansas as well as while in the White House, it was clear that she preferred a more professional position. Other First Ladies have been advocates embracing so-called feminine causes such as literacy or the environment. These First Ladies moved beyond the hostess role but did not go as far as those who became politicos, such as Betty Ford, Rosalynn Carter, and of course, Hillary Clinton.[15] First Ladies acting in the politico realm have a real impact on policy. Many First Ladies took on all three roles, while others were more restrictive in their activities. Of the most recent First Ladies, it was probably Barbara Bush who took the most limited approach to her interpretation of her responsibilities. And, it was Hillary Clinton who broadened the role the most (although it should be noted that Betty Ford actively lobbied on behalf of the Equal Rights Amendment and even admitted to using "'pillow talk' to persuade the president to her point of view."[16]

Mrs. Clinton's desired role as a First Lady involved in the policy-making process was never entirely realized in the way the Clintons had imagined. The press was extremely critical of Mrs. Clinton as First Lady. Research by Shawn Parry-Giles indicates that Mrs. Clinton was subject to a number of stereotyping strategies by the press.[17] The news media and society in general did not have a preexisting narrative in which to understand a more activist and professionally accomplished First Lady or potential First Lady. It was easy to typecast her as a power-hungry feminist intent on abrogating democracy in order to get something for herself or to benefit feminist causes. It was also easy to use evidence of her indifference to fashion and beauty as another reason to be suspicious of her. After all, what woman in our culture is not interested in fashion and beauty? She was pilloried for knowing what she wanted, having real skills to offer a new administration, and not being much interested in the traditional roles First Ladies often play.[18]

Given the range of roles that First Ladies have played, questions remains about how they are perceived by the public and how those perceptions trickle down and influence presidential evaluations. According to public opinion polling, over half of respondents do not think it is appropriate for First Ladies to actively work to influence governmental policy and instead think they should not move beyond simple ceremonial activities when acting as international surrogates. Hillary Clinton's experience with health care policy certainly confirms these results. The Clintons were criticized by almost everyone for Mrs. Clinton's appointment as head of the president's commission on health care. It is not unusual for presidents to enlist a trusted advisor to head policy-development committees, but it was generally seen as an inappropriate role for the First Lady. However, it is important to note that since the Clintons, the public has come to accept that presidential wives may choose to have their own careers outside of their role as the First Lady. Indeed, when Bob Dole ran for president in 1996, his wife, Elizabeth Dole, clearly stated that she would continue her career if he were elected. And in fact, she went on to become a U.S. senator in 2002. Dick Cheney's wife, Lynne Cheney, has actively continued to pursue her career while her husband serves as vice president, even though her career is connected to the government, where she no doubt has influence. Thus, while outside careers are considered acceptable by the public, the appearance of undue influence by an unelected individual on governmental policy, such as in Mrs. Clinton's case, is not. The public was apparently not ready for Bill Clinton's concept of a two-for-one presidency.

Hillary Clinton's popularity with the public was directly affected by how they viewed her activities. Those who thought that she was involved in inappropriate activities for a First Lady were less likely to rate her positively. Interestingly, this was not a simple function of partisanship. In other words, it was not just Republicans who evaluated her on the basis of the kinds of activities in which she was engaged. Democrats also made evaluations based on the acceptability of her activities, rather than giving simple partisan responses. These evaluations in turn had their own independent effect on how the president was perceived. Even when the

Clinton campaign in 1996 tried to remove the presence of Hillary Clinton from the trail and have her maintain a low profile, evaluations of her as First Lady were still an independent factor in how individuals voted in the campaign. Just as the public perception of whether the economy is strong or weak affects voting outcomes, so does the public perception of the First Lady. Only partisanship and the effect of the candidate were stronger factors.[19]

This area of research provides new insight into how the spouse of the president makes a difference in her own right on voting outcomes and perceptions of the president himself. As we move farther into the twenty-first century, we are seeing increasing changes in the roles of women. This will no doubt continue to spill over into the role of the First Lady. While there will always be those women who choose to focus more on the hostess role (certainly Laura Bush appears to prefer this role, while also following in her mother-in-law's footsteps by being an advocate for literacy), there will no doubt be more women who decide to maintain their own careers regardless of their new home address. Even more intriguing is the question of what first husbands will do in office as well as how they will be perceived by the public. With Hillary Clinton having declared her intention to run for the presidency, we may have an opportunity to explore these questions sooner than expected.

IN OFFICE

Perhaps one of the events that Hillary Clinton is most known for during the eight-year administration of her husband was her role with the health care task force. While the famous note posted in Bill Clinton's war room (the location of his campaign headquarters for his 1992 election) was "the economy, stupid," the corollary part was health care. There was growing consensus in the public that America's health care system was broken and needed repair. There were millions of working Americans who simply could not afford health insurance, guaranteeing them a second-class experience. While the United States is known for excellent medical care and state-of-the-art facilities, it is not known for extending access to that care to the entire population. Each year, a larger percentage of the population goes uninsured or underinsured.

During the 1992 campaign, Bill Clinton talked about the need for fixing the health care system and promised that it would be one of the first issues he would tackle when he took office. He did just that, and as was the case with education in Arkansas, he put his wife in charge of the task force. Bill Clinton was not the first president to be concerned about the accessibility of health care to U.S. citizens. Even Richard Nixon was talking about the issue in the 1970s. Bill Clinton was successful at getting health care back in the public spotlight. At the start of the 1992 presidential campaign, few people listed access to decent, affordable health care as one of the most important public-policy issues facing the nation. By inauguration day, it was on the top ten—thanks, in part, to the Clinton campaign's focus on the issue. Since Bill Clinton, all presidential candidates have come up with a health care plan, and there has not been a presidential debate series where candidates were not forced to answer questions about how they would like to address health care for the United States. It is expected to be a major issue again in the 2008 campaign.[20] The challenges of creating a workable health plan for the majority of U.S. citizens are myriad. There are cost impediments as well as ideological impediments having to do not only with whether it is an appropriate role for government and the size and scope of government, but also with how to deliver health care in a decent and affordable way.

The Clintons' intention was to have Mrs. Clinton spearhead a team of experts to develop a new health care policy similar to the way she led the cause for education reform in Arkansas. During the campaign, the idea of Hillary Clinton taking on a major policy role was openly discussed. There was even talk of her receiving a cabinet-level position should Bill Clinton win the election. Most assumed that Hillary would not be a First Lady in the traditional fashion; rather, she would advance the role played by Eleanor Roosevelt and be a serious player. Health care was her opportunity to show what she could accomplish. She had the credentials and abilities to make a huge impact on the direction the government would take on this important issue.

President Clinton pushed for quick action on health care, even promising a bill within his first 100 days in office. While there is a certain logic to this approach, most notably acting before the vast majority of those in favor of maintaining the status quo could themselves galvanize in opposition, the American system of democracy is not known for speed and efficiency. The very system of our government is designed to be slow and deliberate. The president has his own authority and inherent powers of his office, while the legislative body is divided into two separate chambers, the House and Senate. Deliberation slows things down considerably in the legislative process. Major new policy initiatives that mean considerable spending packages and the creation of new levels of bureaucracy are hard to get passed in any event. Any effort to radically change the status quo with regard to health care (or any other issue) was likely to face obstacles. In addition, the decision to place Hillary Clinton in charge of the task force was a fundamental problem that was only compounded by her own mistakes as she went through the policy-making process.

In attempting to develop a new health care policy, Mrs. Clinton adapted the model that was used in Arkansas to reform the education system. First, she used her team of experts to apprise her of the complexity of the issue. Then she went on a listening tour across the country, in which she stopped in to learn firsthand what the challenges were to decent and affordable health care by region. She also spoke to relevant constituency groups, like doctors, insurance companies, and hospital associations.[21] Early news stories of the process were generally positive, often expressing a surprised tone regarding the First Lady's competence and professionalism. At the same time, there was also a counter tone fueled by political opponents that cropped up regarding her motivations and personality flaws.[22] In general, the commission was constantly under scrutiny, and political opponents seized every opportunity to undermine its efforts at health care reform.

To most observers, Mrs. Clinton began her health care reform efforts on the right foot. She arranged for private meetings with many key Republican officials as well as representatives of the health care industry, testified before multiple congressional committees, and addressed the public through a variety of forums—all in an apparent effort to gain momentum and broad support. However, the process by which she developed her ideas for reform was eventually considered flawed. While the official task force was composed of 12 people headed up by liberal Ira Magaziner—the student graduation speaker highlighted with Hillary Clinton in 1969 by *Life*—there was a very large unofficial task force of 500 individuals. This unofficial task force was divided up into 34 different subcommittees, each of which had to report directly to Magaziner. Magaziner reported directly to Mrs. Clinton.[23] The accusation was levied that the process was deceptive in many ways and that the First Lady and Magaziner knew from the start what they wanted but had to go through a false process of listening to people.[24]

The membership of the unofficial task force was initially kept secret. The purported intent was to protect the membership from being lobbied by those interested in the reform process. However, there was a backlash to this level of secrecy, especially from those who were excluded—most notably members of the American Medical Association who were unlikely to be supportive of the single-payer plan, which would have required everyone to enroll in health maintenance organizations (HMOs). The secrecy of the membership ultimately became the subject of a lawsuit filed in federal court to require the release of names. The White House lost its efforts to protect secrecy, in part because the head of the commission (Mrs. Clinton) was not a public employee whose chain of command ended with the president. The efforts to defend the secrecy further enraged the public with regard to Mrs. Clinton, because sometimes the White House made the case that she had an official position and so executive privilege was at issue and other times that she had no official position. The public posturing was confusing to people and gave the impression that the Clintons were trying to cover something up.[25] Neither Hillary Clinton nor Magaziner, an author of books on industrial policy and someone who had worked on health care reform in the state of Rhode Island, had any real experience in creating and passing major national initiatives. Mrs. Clinton's experience in Arkansas, a small state where the number of voters the Clintons had to sway was in the hundreds of thousands rather than hundreds of millions, did not prove to be adequate experience.

Equally problematic was the exclusion of more moderate Republicans who were sympathetic to substantial health care reform. Some argue that Mrs. Clinton assumed that she did not need the votes from the minority party and, as a result, could afford to exclude their input. However, the approach that she wanted to take was essentially for universal health coverage supplied exclusively by the federal government. Many Democrats were leery of this approach as well and frustrated by the apparent unwillingness of Hillary Clinton to compromise her views. At the same time, jokes about the Clinton marriage and who really dominated the relationship were a growing part of late-night television. Not only were opponents critical, but the news media were picking up the mantra and popular media followed with their version.[26] The White House tried to counter the mediated constructions of the First Lady by allowing her to do special one-on-one feature interviews covering her whole life— mother, career woman, hostess, and so forth. However, the efforts were not adequate to tame the maelstrom.

Mrs. Clinton's failure to produce a health care reform package within the 100 days committed to by President Clinton hurt his wife's reputation within Washington. Part of the reason for the delay had to do with the complexity of the plan. The other reason for the delay had to do with damage control in other policy areas that the White House was committed to. The ambitious policy agenda that the First Lady argued for in January proved difficult to manage. Early in 1993, the president failed to pass his economic stimulus package when bipartisan opposition in the Senate filibustered the bill. The failure of the economic package necessarily meant that the health care plan could not be introduced since there would be no way to fund the initiative. In addition, the White House also faced embarrassment over the policy of allowing homosexuals to serve in the military. While allowing homosexuals to serve openly in the military was a popular campaign issue, the White House failed to create the necessary support in Washington to make this change happen. When key military and congressional leaders like General Colin Powell and Senator Sam Nunn (D-GA) came out in opposition to allowing homosexuals to serve openly, public support quickly withered. One of President Clinton's challenges with regard to the gays in the military issue was his lack of legitimacy regarding military issues. This perception was based on the fact that he had not served in the military and that there was evidence from his past that he took pains to try to avoid service. The president ended up compromising with the less than popular "don't ask, don't tell" policy, which neither advocates or opponents were satisfied with.

Publicly, these losses as well as renewed allegations regarding the Whitewater investment deal and Mrs. Clinton's commodities investments of the 1990s sent the president's approval ratings into a downward spiral. President Clinton had the fastest three-month loss of public approval of any president on record.[27] The White House also needed to devote attention to other issues like the ratification of the North American Free Trade Agreement (NAFTA). NAFTA, negotiated during the Bush presidency, would open up commerce restrictions between the United States, Canada, and Mexico. While it was true that President Clinton was ambivalent about the plan, he had spoken in favor of the agreement during the campaign and felt the need to see the trade agreement ratified. During the campaign, he also vowed to negotiate subsequent side agreements on labor and environmental issues.[28] When he came to office, he found that the foreign policy community as well as many White House advisors strongly favored the plan. In the meantime, between the November election and the summer of 1993, organized labor and the environmental movement were able to organize their opposition and had drawn rigid lines in the sand. Ross Perot added to the fray by funding his own anti-NAFTA campaign replete with famous quotes about the giant sucking sound that represented jobs leaving the United States. While Democrats in Congress did not represent unified opposition, too high a percentage opposed the treaty. Many Rust Belt and urban Democrats refused to sign on to the plan, fearing a backlash by organized labor, which they depended on for endorsements and campaign support. Republicans in Congress were more likely to support the agreement, but some had been scared by Perot's campaign, and others were ambivalent about handing Bill Clinton a success—especially one negotiated by his Republican predecessor.[29] While it is clear that Mrs. Clinton did not play a public role in the negotiations over NAFTA, it is also clear that she played some role behind the scenes during the effort to ratify the treaty. Her advice on NAFTA during strategy sessions was to go head to head with the unions. She pointed to her and her husband's experience over the education reform battle in Arkansas by arguing that "[y]ou show people you are willing to fight when you fight with your friends."[30] This was a risky maneuver since the White House also desperately needed to have organized labor's support for the health care plan that was soon to be unveiled. Many efforts were made after NAFTA was ratified to be conciliatory to the labor movement, including seating the aging president of the AFL-CIO next to the First Lady during the 1994 State of the Union address.[31]

In addition to the battle over NAFTA, by September of 1993, the White House found itself trying to recover from the slump in opinion polls, negotiating a peace accord between Israelis and Palestinians, as well as pursuing health care and the vice president's plan for a leaner and more efficient federal government. So a decision was made to table the health care plan announcement until later in the month, because it was felt that the White House could not handle another major policy campaign at the time.[32]

While the press was initially intolerant of Mrs. Clinton's role in creating health care policy, her excessive paranoia about secrecy and the initial exclusion of the media ultimately turned them against her, exacerbating their already contentious relationship. This pattern, which began during the campaign, would last throughout the Clinton administration. Mrs. Clinton suspected that the press had an underlying motive to embarrass or harm her, and as a result she consistently reacted with secrecy and hostility. Her general distrust of the press helped to create a bad relationship between the White House and the press early on.[33]

While it is hard to say what, exactly, the First Lady's role was with regard to the way the Clinton administration conducted public-policy business, it was clear from the start that the press would be treated differently than they had become accustomed to in the past. The White House Press Corps was initially denied a great deal of access that it had previously been used to—not just on health care, but on all other issues as well. The White House adopted a strategy used during the campaign of bypassing the Washington press corps and relying on alternative sources like local news media outlets, having representatives like James Carville spend time on cable news shows and talk radio. What worked during the campaign did not work well as a governing style. This approach to the press created a poor initial relationship between the White House and the press corps, which was used to being treated with great respect. This situation probably had something to do with the president's dramatic 24-point drop in his approval ratings during his first three months in office. In that time period, only 21 percent of television news reporters' comments about the president were positive. As a point of reference, during President Bush's initial three months in office in 1989, 74 percent of television news comments were positive.[34]

Perhaps a more open approach with the press would have saved the administration considerable trouble. Some analysts blame the relative youth and inexperience of both the Clintons and White House staff for creating the bad press relationship.[35] Certainly, a more cooperative approach on health care would have been beneficial. Politics is often the art of compromise. Few, if any, substantial successes occur by digging in one's heels. It is likely that simply by virtue of appearing unwilling to bend, the opposition grows larger. The Clintons both failed to court those who most need to be courted in Washington, Congress, powerful interest groups, and the press.[36] The result was a reputation for being inflexible and having a superiority complex. Their general approach won the Clintons few friends in Washington, even among congressional Democrats, and resulted in President Clinton's health care proposal arriving DOA on the steps of the Capitol.

Needless to say, delays in producing a plan, combined with the complexities of the proposed plan, the time-consuming process of getting legislation through Congress, and the cost to the nation, meant that opponents had a chance to get organized and run a successful public relations campaign against the proposal. One group of opponents, the Health Insurance Association of America, developed and aired the now famous Harry and Louise ads, which were short commercials that depicted a middle-aged white couple denouncing the evils of a managed care system by preying on people's fears that they would have less than adequate care.[37] While these ads went out to only a relatively small viewing audience, the media picked up on the theme and began to investigate the question of whether managed care was right for the United States. Concurrently, Elizabeth McCaughey of the conservative Manhattan Institute went public with her think-tank analysis of the plan, which raised many of the same concerns.[38] Public approval quickly began to wane. Concurrently, Congress was failing to act in a unified way. Relevant committees were not reporting bills that adequately reflected the White House proposal.[39] Once public opinion for a federal health plan turned negative, it was just a matter of time before Congress killed the legislation.[40]

Mrs. Clinton's problems did not end with her aborted attempt to pass fundamental change in the health care system. Indeed, that was only the tip of the iceberg. Perhaps one of the greatest problems that she faced while her husband was in office was the couple's investment in Whitewater back when she and Bill Clinton lived in Arkansas. The Whitewater issue surfaced during the campaign and came back to haunt the couple during the president's first year in office. Whitewater was a land investment made with the McDougals, old friends and political supporters of the Clintons. A fairly complicated land-development deal, Whitewater raised questions regarding the Clintons' investment, their connection to a failed savings and loan, and whether or not they had received special treatment while Bill was governor. The Clintons always proclaimed their innocence of any wrongdoing, highlighting the fact that they lost money on the real-estate venture.

The timing of the interest in Whitewater could not have been worse for the Clintons and their goal of reforming the health care system. An independent counsel was appointed by Attorney General Janet Reno to investigate Whitewater. However, the independent counsel was not actually necessary. At the time, there was no legal requirement to appoint a special prosecutor, and in fact, Hillary Clinton vigorously opposed it. She felt that appointing an independent counsel would only invite an extended investigation into the Clintons' private affairs. However, many people, including George Stephanopolous, a senior White House advisor, argued equally forcefully in favor of making the appointment as a means of putting an end to the ongoing perception of a scandal-ridden administration.[41] Moreover, it was suggested that the attention being paid to Whitewater was harmful to President Clinton's ability to fulfill his agenda. The hope was that the appointment of an independent counsel would take the oxygen out of the scandal and allow for renewed focus on health care.[42] While there is logic to this argument, it eventually backfired, and Hillary Clinton's fears proved true, with an independent counsel investigation that persisted through much of the two Clinton administrations and led to endless depositions and time spent answering questions about events from the past. Ultimately, the investigation also led to the impeachment of the president and charges unrelated to Whitewater or any other financial dealings.

Compounding the problems facing the Clintons was Vince Foster's suicide while working for the new administration. Foster was a former partner of the Rose Law Firm and a close friend and counsel to the Clintons. At Hillary Clinton's request, he left Arkansas to join the administration, despite the fact that he was not all that interested in doing so.[43] However, he had long been a staunch and loyal friend of the First Lady's, and she was able to persuade him that she needed his help. Unfortunately, he was clearly out of his league, unfamiliar with the inner workings of Washington and the detailed ethics laws by which government workers must live—he was the quintessential outsider when the Clintons most needed a savvy insider. He further compounded his problems, and those of Mrs. Clinton, by hiring another former Arkansan when he needed help with the workload, rather than taking the opportunity to find someone who was more familiar with the ways of Washington.[44] Many observers suggest that the pressure finally became too much for Foster, driving him to commit suicide. It is impossible, however, to know why Foster really took his own life. He did not leave behind any record other than a crumpled and cryptic note. Foster's death is reported to have had a profound effect on the Clintons, who valued their friend and were devastated by his death.[45]

After the failure of the health care proposal, Mrs. Clinton publicly took a more traditional role in the administration. She kept her West Wing offices but no longer had an official role as policy developer. While it is known that the First Lady was a crucial advisor to the president, forging a strong relationship with many of his closest advisors, it is not easy to assess the precise role that she played. An article on Senator Clinton's position on the Iraq War indicates that she was a key and influential proponent of Clinton's use of force in the Balkans.[46] While the failure of reforming health care made it difficult to justify having Mrs. Clinton continue in such a public arena, few doubt that she was a force behind the scenes. However, she was no longer going to be placed front and center of future policy endeavors.

NEW CONGRESSIONAL LEADERSHIP

By 1995, many people thought Bill Clinton's presidency was doomed. The Democratic Party lost its majority status in both the House and the Senate in 1994, putting the Republicans in charge for the first time in 40 years. The so-called Republican revolution of 1994 was orchestrated largely by Republican Newt Gingrich, who would take over as Speaker of the House in 1995. The plan for taking back both houses of Congress rested on a deep candidate recruitment effort, a common message articulated through the Contract with America and a set of weekly training tapes to make sure that candidates remained consistently on message and consistent with the national news effort on issues like welfare reform, taxes, and abortion.[47] In 1995 the government shut down several different times as the president and Congress could not agree on a budget spending bill—a clash over the differences between the status quo and the Contract with America. The Republicans thought that the blame would ultimately be passed onto the president, which encouraged them to hold fast and not compromise, but their hard-line position backfired. President

Clinton was seen as the one who was willing to come to some agreement, while the Republicans were perceived as the recalcitrant ones.

Finally, President Clinton turned once again to Dick Morris, a political consultant who had helped him with earlier campaigns in Arkansas. Morris suggested an approach of triangulation, whereby the president co-opted traditional Republican issues, such as welfare reform. Bill Clinton firmly approached new policy initiatives from a centrist perspective and managed to succeed both legislatively and in his quest for reelection.

Some analysis of Bill Clinton's first term indicates that legislatively he was enormously successful. In fact, for his first term, he holds one of the highest legislative success scores of any president in the modern era.[48] This record is due, at least in part, to the urgings of the First Lady to take on an ambitious legislative plan. In addition, there is some evidence that the Republican revolution itself contributed to Bill Clinton's success. In the second half of the first term, the president faced strong opposition in Congress, but he had the advantage of being a single voice on issues that mattered to him, while the Congress was represented by more than 500 voices. This rhetorical advantage helps presidents a great deal in their quest for policy success. Some also argue that the change in Congress forced the White House to stay more directed and on message.[49] While Clinton's approval ratings plummeted after his first three months in office, they generally saw a steady trend upward after the Republicans took control of Congress. The public did not respond well to the aggressive nature of the congressional leadership in pursuing its agenda.[50] The Republican leadership, including an excitable Newt Gingrich and the gravelly voiced Bob Dole, was less charismatic to the public when compared with the affable and collegial president.

During the second half of the first term, Mrs. Clinton remained largely out of the public eye with regard to public policy. In a public statement early in 1995, it was reported

> She intends, Hillary Clinton said, to pursue her long-standing interests in women, children and health in another realm, concentrating less on legislation and more on the bully pulpit, hoping that she can be defined by what she talks about. She plans to write more articles like one she penned for *Newsweek* recently regarding orphanages and the treatment of children in the welfare debate.[51]

In choosing issue advocacy more oriented on public awareness, such as advocating for women to get mammograms, the First Lady was signaling that she understood that she could not take on roles where she would be seen by the public as shaping policy. There is little doubt that she remained involved in policy development as well as strategic planning, but it is difficult to say just what her role was. Her West Wing office and staff stayed in place. Her chief of staff remained an advisor to the president.

A large percentage of the news coverage of Mrs. Clinton in 1995 and 1996 centered on accusations regarding the Whitewater land deal, her commodities investments, and pieces about her international travel and campaign stops. Her international travel included a well-received address at the International Conference on Women in Beijing in 1995 and a popular trip with daughter Chelsea to India. On some of these travel and campaign stops, Mrs. Clinton even gave a glimpse of a perhaps more policy-active First Lady than the public knew about. For instance, in a visit to Thailand, she told a group of women that she met with that she would not "put a bag over my head.... I'm just going to keep doing what I have been doing... which is to just say what I mean and work on what I care about."[52]

NOTES

1. Bob Woodward, *The Agenda: Inside the Clinton White House* (New York: Simon and Schuster, 1994); Elizabeth Drew, *On the Edge: The Clinton Presidency* (New York: Simon and Schuster, 1995).

2. Elizabeth Drew, *On the Edge: The Clinton Presidency* (New York: Simon and Schuster, 1995).

3. Ibid.

4. Ibid.

5. Ibid.

6. Ibid.

7. Ibid., p. 260.

8. Stanley A. Renshon, *High Hopes: The Clinton Presidency and the Politics of Ambition* (New York: Routledge, 1998).

9. Ibid.

10. Bob Woodward, *The Agenda: Inside the Clinton White House* (New York: Simon and Schuster, 1994).

11. Ibid.

12. Robert P. Watson, "Source Material: Toward the Study of the First Lady: The State of Scholarship," *Presidential Studies Quarterly* 33, no. 2 (June 2003): 423–41.

13. Charles Tien, Regan Checchio, and Arthur H. Miller, "The Impact of First Wives on Presidential Campaigns and Elections," in *Women in Politics: Outsiders or Insiders*, 3rd ed., ed. Lois Duke-Whitaker (Upper Saddle River, N.J.: Prentice Hall, 1999), pp. 149–68.

14. Ibid.

15. Ibid.

16. Ibid.

17. Shawn Parry-Giles, "Mediating Hillary Rodham Clinton: Television News Practices and Image-Making in the Postmodern Age," *Critical Studies in Media Communication* 17, no. 2 (June 2000): 205–26.

18. Ibid.

19. Charles Tien, Regan Checchio, and Arthur H. Miller, "The Impact of First Wives on Presidential Campaigns and Elections," in *Women in Politics: Outsiders or Insiders*, 3rd ed., ed. Lois Duke-Whitaker (Upper Saddle River, N.J.: Prentice Hall, 1999), pp. 149–68.

20. Jonathan Cohn, "The Health Care Plan That Dare Not Speak Its Name," *The New Republic*, June 4, 2007, pp. 24–28.

21. Elizabeth Drew, *On the Edge: The Clinton Presidency* (New York: Simon and Schuster, 1995).

22. Shawn Parry-Giles, "Mediating Hillary Rodham Clinton: Television News Practices and Image-Making in the Postmodern Age," *Critical Studies in Media Communication* 17, no. 2 (June 2000): 205–26.

23. Elizabeth Drew, *On the Edge: The Clinton Presidency* (New York: Simon and Schuster, 1995).

24. Bob Woodward, *The Agenda: Inside the Clinton White House* (New York: Simon and Schuster, 1994); Elizabeth Drew, *On the Edge: The Clinton Presidency* (New York: Simon and Schuster, 1995).

25. Paul J. Quirk and Joseph Hichliffe, "Domestic Policy: The Trials of a Centrist Democracy," in *The Clinton Presidency*, ed. Colin Campbell and Bert A. Rockman (Chatham, N.J.: Chatham House Publishers, 1996), pp. 262–89.

26. Nathan Cobb, "The Hillary Jokes—Not Everyone Is Laughing," *Boston Globe*, April 6, 1993, p. 1.

27. William W. Lammers and Michael Genovese, *The Presidency and Domestic Policy: Comparing Leadership Styles, FDR to Clinton* (Washington, D.C.: CQ Press, 2000).

28. Barbara Sinclair, "Trying to Govern Positively in a Negative Era," in *The Clinton Presidency*, ed. Colin Campbell and Bert A. Rockman (Chatham, N.J.: Chatham House Publishers, 1996), pp. 88–125.

29. Ibid.

30. Graham K. Wilson, "The Clinton Administration and Interest Groups," in *The Clinton Presidency*, ed. Colin Campbell and Bert A. Rockman (Chatham, N.J.: Chatham House Publishers, 1996), pp. 212–33.

31. Ibid.

32. Barbara Sinclair, "Trying to Govern Positively in a Negative Era," in *The Clinton Presidency*, ed. Colin Campbell and Bert A. Rockman (Chatham, N.J.: Chatham House Publishers, 1996), pp. 88–125.

33. Stanley A. Renshon, *High Hopes: The Clinton Presidency and the Politics of Ambition* (New York: Routledge, 1998).

34. William W. Lammers and Michael Genovese, *The Presidency and Domestic Policy: Comparing Leadership Styles, FDR to Clinton* (Washington, D.C.: CQ Press, 2000).

35. Ibid.

36. Gail Sheehy, *Hillary's Choice* (New York: Random House, 1999).

37. William W. Lammers and Michael Genovese, *The Presidency and Domestic Policy: Comparing Leadership Styles, FDR to Clinton* (Washington, D.C.: CQ Press, 2000).

38. Jonathan Cohn, "The Health Care Plan That Dare Not Speak Its Name," *The New Republic*, June 4, 2007, pp. 24–28.

39. Barbara Sinclair, "Trying to Govern Positively in a Negative Era," in *The Clinton Presidency*, ed. Colin Campbell and Bert A. Rockman (Chatham, N.J.: Chatham House Publishers, 1996), pp. 88–125.

40. Elizabeth Drew, *On the Edge: The Clinton Presidency* (New York: Simon and Schuster, 1995).

41. Ibid.

42. Ibid.

43. Ibid.

44. Joyce Milton, *The First Partner: Hillary Rodham Clinton* (New York: William Morrow and Company, 1999).

45. Stanley A. Renshon, *High Hopes: The Clinton Presidency and the Politics of Ambition* (New York: Routledge, 1998).

46. Michael Crowley, "Hillary's War: The Real Reason She Won't Apologize," *The New Republic*, April 2, 2007, pp. 19–25.

47. Conne Bruck and Anita Kunz, "The Politics of Perception," *The New Yorker*, October 9, 1995, pp. 50–78.

48. William W. Lammers and Michael Genovese, *The Presidency and Domestic Policy: Comparing Leadership Styles, FDR to Clinton* (Washington, D.C.: CQ Press, 2000).

49. Stanley A. Renshon, *High Hopes: The Clinton Presidency and the Politics of Ambition* (New York: Routledge, 1998).

50. Scott Keeter, "Public Opinion and the Election," in *The Election of 1996: Reports and Interpretations*, ed. Gerald Pomper (Chatham, N.J.: Chatham House, 1996), pp. 107–33.

51. David Maraniss, "First Lady of Paradox," *The Washington Post*, January 15, 1995, p. A1.

52. John F. Harris, "First Lady Still Interpreting Her Role," *The Washington Post*, November 27, 1996, p. A1.

Chapter 6

THE 1996 ELECTION AND THE SECOND TERM

REELECTION

Running for president as an incumbent and running as a challenger are two substantially different tasks. There are several key advantages to incumbency: name recognition, presidential image, record in office (if it is good), and being a so-called known quantity (people know what to expect and so feel secure with the incumbent). The challenges that incumbents generally face are ongoing criticism in the media, a public mood that distrusts Washington insiders and politicians generally (a legacy, in part, of the Watergate scandal), and promises from the first election that may not have been met.[1]

As a challenger in 1992, Bill Clinton was able to capitalize on a poor economy, a relatively strong third-party candidate (Perot) who split the vote, and the long-term Washington insider status of the sitting president to win the election. As an incumbent, Bill Clinton was the insider. Although the economy in 1996 was doing well, President Clinton faced a myriad of potential challenges:

1. The administration struggled early on with certain policy issues that tainted public opinion. His approval ratings, while generally positive, were not high. During the summer of 1996, less than 60 percent of the public approved of the job Bill Clinton was doing as president.[2]
2. While he had been legislatively successful in a general sense, there were a few key losses, like health care and gays in the military, which were likely to follow him through the campaign.

3. The country had shown at least some affinity for Republican ideology during the 1994 election, which brought Republican control to both houses of Congress for the first time in over 30 years. The Republican Congress made an effort to obstruct as many Clinton administration policies as it could.
4. There was an ongoing furor over Bill and Hillary Clinton's financial dealings in Arkansas, including an investigation by a special prosecutor.
5. A woman named Paula Jones had brought a sexual harassment complaint against the president.

The two Democratic presidents prior to Bill Clinton (Johnson and Carter) were not reelected. Johnson removed himself from consideration in part because he faced serious challenges within his own party, and Carter lost his reelection bid in part due to challenges within his own party that raised serious questions about his leadership ability. The challenger, Ronald Reagan, successfully continued the tone of criticism from the primaries into the general election. In order to avoid the past, especially in the wake of seemingly endless legislative challenges from the Republican Congress, the Clintons adopted the strategy of raising as many funds as they possibly could as early as they could. The thought was that this fund-raising strategy would effectively deter challengers, and it did.[3] Bill Clinton faced no serious challenge in 1996 from other Democrats.

Bill Clinton's Republican opponent in 1996 was Bob Dole, the majority leader in the U.S. Senate. Also in the race was Ross Perot. Since some felt that Perot's presence in the 1992 campaign had hurt Bush's chance for reelection, the Dole campaign was able to successfully keep Perot in the rear of the pack by excluding him from the presidential debates. Perot's only way of reaching voters was advertising, but his exclusion from the public forum during the 1992 campaign, as well as his mysterious dropping out of the race and subsequent return, made him less legitimate in the eyes of the public.[4] Dole was tainted by precampaign coverage of Congress during the budget battles with the president. In addition, the White House was able to successfully play on the age difference between the president at 50 and Dole at 73.[5]

Unlike the 1992 election, the role of Mrs. Clinton was considerably less visible.[6] Several months before the campaign was underway, the First Lady essentially disappeared from view. When she reemerged, it was as a more traditional wife, traveling with her daughter and publicizing the publication of her book It Takes a Village. Hillary Clinton was never destined to take a passive role while the wife of the president. Although she faded into the background during reelection, she did continue to push for the interests of women and children, issues on which she had long been focused. While she did not completely disappear behind the scenes, she was not the presence she had been in the 1992 campaign.

After the 1994 congressional elections, the Clintons asked a friend from their Arkansas days, political consultant Dick Morris, to step in to plan the reelection campaign. Morris's advice sometimes proved controversial, such as telling the president to take more conservative positions on issues than his staff thought necessary. The result was growing dissent within the White House. In order to counter the tone of dissent within his own administration, President Clinton held weekly strategy meetings with Morris, the White House staff, and the vice president. Mrs. Clinton did not attend those meetings because it was felt that if the public learned of her presence, there would be the perception that she was once again using her role as First Lady inappropriately to achieve a political end.[7] Excluding Mrs. Clinton from those strategy meetings was a direct result of the health care debacle and the ongoing investigation into the Whitewater land deal. Without a doubt, Mrs. Clinton bumped into the limits to which she could push the boundaries of the role of the First Lady with her attempts at health care reform.

In keeping with the more traditional role of First Ladies, Mrs. Clinton did address the Democratic Convention in 1996. In that speech, introducing her husband, the First Lady spoke about raising her child, community generally, and her husband. It was staid and demur and did not advocate for any particular political agenda. That speech received very positive reviews from the media.[8]

Bill Clinton handily won reelection from challengers Bob Dole and Ross Perot in 1996. This victory, in part, was the result of the president being able to successfully dominate the news coverage during the campaign. He was aided in this effort by the media itself when the networks decided to scale back coverage of the 1996 campaign in an effort to boost ratings.[9] Bill Clinton won the 1996 election with 49.2 percent of the vote. Dole took 40.8 percent of the vote, and Perot 8.5 percent.

Throughout both his terms of office, Bill Clinton took on a complex legislative agenda and tended to this agenda personally. President Clinton set up regular meetings with members of Congress, made many phone calls to members of Congress, and even visited the Capitol more often than most presidents. At the same time, he also took his policy agenda public at every opportunity. This attention to detail was probably the chief reason why he was one of the most legislatively successful presidents in history.[10] Just before the 1996 election, President Clinton pushed Congress into passing a welfare reform bill. This move frustrated many staff members and members of his cabinet who felt that the legislation, while making some positive changes, was leaving the poor without a safety net. They charged President Clinton with signing the bill to help ensure his reelection, rather than caring about good policy.[11]

After the election, Mrs. Clinton retained her low public profile on policy issues. She did keep her West Wing office. During the second term, Mrs. Clinton hired a new chief of staff, Melanne Verveer. In keeping with Mrs. Clinton's distrust of outsiders, Verveer was an old and trusted friend.[12] In 1997, Mrs. Clinton continued her travels to places important to the Clinton administration's foreign policy goals. She also hosted a conference on child-care issues in October of that year.[13] The emphasis on child care for this conference is interesting in terms of giving outside viewers a look at the role she might have played behind the scenes. While Hillary Clinton apparently did not take part in any role to create legislation on child-care issues, child care was one of the issues that President Clinton indicated was a problem with the welfare reform bill passed in 1996. Upon signing the legislation, the president acknowledged that he considered it a starting point, not a finished product. There was some speculation after the president was reelected that the First Lady might try to take a formal role—one in which she reported to the president—in welfare reform, but that idea was rejected publicly by White House staff.[14]

While not specifically playing a policy role for the White House, Mrs. Clinton continued to show glimpses of certain behind-the-scenes influences, often speaking publicly about her position on issues and sometimes urging the public to consider her point of view. For instance, in one press conference that involved her and some senior White House staff appearing together, Mrs. Clinton urged the public to lend greater support for foreign aid. She argued that it was imperative to increase foreign aid as a way of encouraging other nations to take better care of their citizenry, fight epidemics of disease, decrease terrorism, and promote peace generally.[15] Another glimpse of Mrs. Clinton's influence came in 1998 when, during a tour of Central America, she announced an increase in aid to Central American nations that were devastated by Hurricane Mitch.[16] She also publicly stated that she felt it in the long-term interest of peace in the Middle East for the Palestinian people to have their own state.[17]

One trend that is abundantly clear regarding the First Lady's role in the White House during the second term is that she became more interested and involved in foreign policy. Not only did she visit many foreign nations, but she often went without her husband (but did take her daughter, Chelsea) and advocated for specific policy while abroad. A recent article about Mrs. Clinton's interest and expertise in foreign policy documents both a close relationship with Secretary of State Madeleine Albright (another Wellesley graduate), as well as her influence regarding foreign policy. For instance, when President Clinton had to make the difficult choice of whether or not to intervene militarily in the Balkans, it is clear that Mrs. Clinton was in favor of the intervention and pushed her husband to undertake it.[18]

Any examination of the life of Hillary Rodham Clinton needs to acknowledge that while First Lady, Mrs. Clinton remained as busy as she could be. She showed herself to be a valiant supporter of causes that were important to her, and when the public expressed a frustration with a First Lady who had a formal policy-making role in the White House, she found a way to influence policy that was more palatable to the citizenry of the United States.

After the election, most would have thought that the Clinton presidency was home free. However, the new term brought more troubles for the administration. The Whitewater investigation brought no charges against the Clintons for impropriety in Arkansas. However, a new scandal emerged in conjunction with that investigation, and by the fall of 1998, the president was facing impeachment charges. Most of the news of 1998 regarding both Clintons surrounded the investigation into Whitewater and President Clinton's relationship with Monica Lewinsky.

MONICA LEWINSKY

While the Clinton administration was beset by numerous scandals, the one that threatened to literally bring down the presidency was President Clinton's relationship with Monica Lewinsky. While it was widely known that President Clinton had a history of extramarital affairs, it was assumed that those days were over—or if they were not, it was certainly the case that no one dreamed the president's behavior could cause his impeachment.

No new accusations of infidelity were raised since the 1992 election, and as far as the media could see, the president appeared to be on best behavior. This was obviously not the case. When the information about his relationship with Lewinsky first came to light, Bill Clinton's initial instinct was to do what had worked so well in the past—to deny the existence of an affair. And Mrs. Clinton did what she had so often done in the past: she defended her husband. In the case of Lewinsky, it was fairly clear that Mrs. Clinton was not initially aware of the relationship. Mrs. Clinton took to the airwaves, stridently denying the relationship and making accusations of a "vast right-wing conspiracy" bent on bringing down her husband's presidency.[19] Perhaps the most egregious aspect of the early response was that Bill Clinton allowed his wife to appear on the *Today* show to vehemently deny a relationship between himself and the intern. Later, Hillary would learn that she had defended her husband despite the truth of the accusations.

The roots of the scandal becoming public date back to the civil suit brought by Paula Jones, a former Arkansas state employee, against President Clinton. She claimed to have been sexually harassed by Bill Clinton when he was still governor of Arkansas. The *American Spectator* had run a story during the 1992 election claiming that Bill Clinton cheated on his wife, and one of the women identified in the story was Paula Jones (although the article did not use her last name). One of the state troopers assigned to Governor Clinton's protection detail claimed that Jones was one of many women brought to the governor for sexual escapades, and that after her initial encounter, Jones stated that she wanted to be Bill Clinton's regular girlfriend.[20] Only after the article was released was it discovered that the state trooper who provided the evidence about the extramarital affairs was disgruntled with then Governor Clinton and was subsequently discredited.

However, Paula Jones claimed that the *American Spectator* article did not sufficiently hide her identity and that her friends and family were able to determine that she was the Paula mentioned in the article. During a convention of the Conservative Political Action Committee, Jones held a press conference publicly identifying herself as the Paula mentioned in the article. She then accused President Clinton of sexually harassing her, and in May 1994, filed suit against him. Rather than settling the case out of court, the Clintons decided to let it go forward. Their reasoning was that if they settled, it would open the door for future claims against Bill Clinton and give credibility to similar stories.[21]

The decision to allow the case to go forward would be one that the Clintons would come to regret.[22] They assumed that the case would be thrown out because Jones never suffered any ill effects. She was not denied a position or held back in any way, nor did she have any evidence of harassment. The Clintons also knew that Jones was being supported by conservative billionaire Richard Mellon Scaife, who very much disliked the president. However, the case did go forward, and the Jones legal team was able to take depositions from witnesses, including President Clinton. It was during this deposition that the president was questioned about a relationship with Monica Lewinsky, which he subsequently denied. It was the possibility that President Clinton committed perjury that formed the basis of the impeachment trial against him. The Whitewater special prosecutor was assigned to investigate these new claims of perjury by Attorney General Janet Reno after he specifically petitioned her to broaden the scope of his investigation.[23] By the end of the investigation, some observers thought that Special Prosecutor Kenneth Starr was on a personal vendetta against the Clintons.

When it became apparent that President Clinton initially lied about his relationship with Lewinsky, Hillary Clinton dealt with the situation much in the same way as she had in the past: privately. However, it should be noted that while she no longer publicly defended her husband, she also never publicly challenged him. Instead, she silently and implicitly defended him by remaining at his side. The media seemed preoccupied with the question of what was going on in the Clintons' relationship. Americans avidly watched for any sign of marital discord but rarely saw anything visible to an outsider. Yet, by her own account, it was one of the most difficult times of her marriage, requiring her to summon all of her inner strength to deal with the most private situation in a most public manner.[24] Adding insult to injury, shortly after President Clinton admitted having an affair with Monica Lewinsky, the Clintons were scheduled to leave for Martha's Vineyard to go on vacation with their daughter, Chelsea. While it was not the relaxing vacation originally intended, it did allow her to escape Washington, D.C., and have time to herself to come to grips with the situation created by her husband. By the end of the summer, she was at least willing to fight for Bill Clinton as president, if not as her husband.[25]

The tale of the affair between the president and the intern has now become legendary in American politics. Not surprisingly, much has been written about Bill Clinton's relationship with Lewinsky. It has earned its place in the history books for launching the first impeachment trial of a president since the 1800s. While he was ultimately impeached by the House of Representatives, the Senate failed to convict him, thereby securing the remainder of his presidency. By February 1999, the matter was resolved by the Senate, and the Clintons could attempt to put it behind them.

It should also be noted that during the entirety of the scandal, public opinion rarely swayed from the Clintons. When news first broke of the president's affair with Lewinsky and that it was likely that he lied about it, President Clinton initially saw a nine-point drop in his presidential approval ratings (to 51% from 60%).[26] After that initial drop, his approval ratings rallied, and he had approval ratings of over 70 percent, some of the highest of any president on record.[27] During the impeachment process in the House of Representatives and through the Senate trial, President Clinton's approval ratings remained in the 60s, and there was never much support for his removal from office. Mrs. Clinton also received high approval ratings in this time period.[28]

This massive outpouring of public support for both the president and the First Lady was likely due to several causes:

1. The economy was strong. Compared to 1992, when Bill Clinton was running for president, the public was much more optimistic than it had been in years about the economic future of the nation.

2. The president generally took popular positions on issues. With the exception of a few issues where he lost big, like health care, his basic inclination toward centrism served him well in the White House.

3. The public found President Clinton charming, while they found little charming about Kenneth Starr, the special prosecutor. The majority of Americans did not trust Kenneth Starr or his investigation.[29]

4. Most Americans felt that the issue was a private one to be dealt with between Bill and Hillary Clinton. It was clear that in many ways, they felt the first couple's pain. One poll in December 1998 indicated that U.S. citizens felt that the best way to avoid scandals like these in the future would be to allow presidents' private lives to remain private, rather than try to elect someone with a high moral character.[30]

THE CLINTONS AS PARENTS

With so much interest in the Clintons' personal and public lives in the press, it is surprising that there was little analysis of their role as parents. Named after a Joni Mitchell song, "Chelsea Morning," Chelsea Clinton has managed to escape excessive media scrutiny. In an era where all aspects of an individual's life seem to be fair game, it is actually quite remarkable that Chelsea Clinton has managed to mostly elude the headlines. The Clintons worked extremely hard to protect their daughter, who was only 12 when Bill Clinton was elected president. The media also deserve some credit for respecting the wishes of the Clintons to maintain their daughter's privacy.

During the Clintons' first term in office, Chelsea attended the private Sidwell Friends School in Washington, D.C., graduating in 1997. She then went to Stanford University, where she earned her bachelor's degree in history. While there was initial interest in her arrival at Stanford, it was not that long after the death of Princess Diana, a time when the media received considerable scrutiny for their part in her car crash. As a result, the media seemed somewhat chastened and more mindful of respecting celebrities like Chelsea. Interestingly, her arrival resulted in the firing of a student reporter who violated the college paper's policy of not reporting stories about Chelsea unless they were news. The reporter wrote about the special efforts taken on behalf of the university to ensure that Chelsea was treated like any other student.[31]

Chelsea Clinton seems to maintain a very positive relationship with both of her parents. She has never spoken publicly about either of them. While still in college, she returned to the White House for the end of her father's presidency. She has traveled extensively with both parents around the world. Indeed, while her mother was busy campaigning for her first Senate election, Chelsea Clinton went to Asia with her father. She also assumed some of the First Lady's hosting responsibilities in the few remaining weeks of the Clinton administration when her mother was already in the Senate.

Following her four years at Stanford, she studied at University College at Oxford where she earned her master's in international relations. Today, Chelsea Clinton lives in Manhattan and works on Wall Street in the financial industry and campaigns with her mother.

LEGACY

Perhaps one of the most important accomplishments of Hillary Clinton during her husband's presidency was changing the role of the First Lady. She was not the first to do so; indeed, most people credit Eleanor Roosevelt with establishing the precedent for a strong First Lady. However, Hillary Clinton did take the position farther than any of her predecessors. While at times it was thought that she took the role too far, she clearly placed her stamp on it. She traveled the world, often served as a surrogate for her husband, helped raise money for the Democratic Party, and eventually launched herself into elected office in her own right. Of course, this does not mean that all subsequent First Ladies will continue in her footsteps. Laura Bush is unlikely to go as far as Hillary Clinton in her activities while being First Lady to President Bush. While Laura Bush is certainly an advocate for literacy, an extension of her career as a teacher and librarian, she has not been a politico. However, the next First Lady to enter office with her own career will likely face less skepticism and criticism due to Hillary Clinton's time in the White House.

Legislatively, the Clinton administration was fairly successful. It was able to pass a large number of policies that were staked out at the beginning of Bill Clinton's presidency. It is easy to note big failures like health care, but in general, there was great success, more success than most presidents have. President Clinton finished his second term with high approval ratings, a booming economy, and a tarnished personal reputation. As promised when the Clinton presidency was over, the time had come for the priority to be Mrs. Clinton's career. Before they moved out of the White House, Hillary Clinton's quest to become a senator from New York began.

NOTES

1. Stephen J. Wayne, *The Road to the White House, 1996* (New York: Simon and Schuster, 1997).

2. Scott Keeter, "Public Opinion and the Election," in *The Election of 1996: Reports and Interpretations*, ed. Gerald Pomper (Chatham, N.J.: Chatham House, 1996), pp. 107–33.

3. Stephen J. Wayne, *The Road to the White House, 1996* (New York: Simon and Schuster, 1997).

4. Marion Just, "Candidate Strategies and the Media Campaign," in *The Election of 1996: Reports and Interpretations*, ed. Gerald Pomper (Chatham, N.J.: Chatham House, 1996), pp. 77–106.

5. Ibid.

6. Charles Tien, Regan Checchio, and Arthur H. Miller, "The Impact of First Wives on Presidential Campaigns and Elections," in *Women in Politics: Outsiders or Insiders*, 3rd ed., ed. Lois Duke-Whitaker (Upper Saddle River, N.J.: Prentice Hall, 1999), pp. 149–68.

7. Stephen J. Wayne, *The Road to the White House, 1996* (New York: Simon and Schuster, 1997).

8. Marion Just, "Candidate Strategies and the Media Campaign," in *The Election of 1996: Reports and Interpretations*, ed. Gerald Pomper (Chatham, N.J.: Chatham House, 1996), pp. 77–106.

9. Ibid.

10. William W. Lammers and Michael Genovese, *The Presidency and Domestic Policy: Comparing Leadership Styles, FDR to Clinton* (Washington, D.C.: CQ Press, 2000).

11. Karen Ball, "Matters of Principle," *The Washington Post*, November 23, 1997, p. W19.

12. Ibid.

13. Katherine Q. Seelye, "Hillary Clinton Begins Drive to Improve Care for Children," *New York Times*, October 1, 1997, p. A20.

14. Todd S. Purdum, "Mrs. Clinton Foresees Role in Welfare Overhaul," *New York Times*, November 25, 1996, p. A12.

15. Thomas W. Lippman, "Hillary Clinton Urges Public to Support Foreign Aid," *The Washington Post*, June 17, 1997, p. A13.

16. "Central America Gets More Help," *Miami Herald*, November 17, 1998, p. A24.

17. Agence France-Presse, "Hillary Clinton Supports a Palestinian State," *New York Times*, May 7, 1998, p. A8.

18. Michael Crowley, "Hillary's War: The Real Reason She Won't Apologize," *The New Republic*, April 2, 2007, pp. 19–25.

19. Jeffrey Toobin, *A Vast Conspiracy* (New York: Random House, 2000).

20. Hillary Rodham Clinton, *Living History* (New York: Simon and Schuster, 2003), p. 227.

21. Ibid.

22. Ibid, p. 440.

23. Michael R. Beschloss, *The Impeachment and Trial of President Clinton* (New York: Times Books, Random House, 1999), p. xv.

24. Hillary Rodham Clinton, *Living History* (New York: Simon and Schuster, 2003), p. 440.

25. Ibid.

26. Molly W. Sonner and Clyde Wilcox, "Forgiving and Forgetting: Public Support for Bill Clinton during the Lewinsky Scandal," *PS: Political Science and Politics* 32, no. 3 (September 1999): 554–57.

27. Ibid.

28. Mary McGrory, "Mr. and Mrs. Comeback Kid," *The Washington Post*, November 8, 1998, p. C1.

29. Molly W. Sonner and Clyde Wilcox, "Forgiving and Forgetting: Public Support for Bill Clinton during the Lewinsky Scandal," *PS: Political Science and Politics* 32, no. 3 (September 1999): 554–57.

30. Ibid.

31. M. L. Stein, "Fired Over Chelsea," *Editor and Publisher Magazine*, October 11, 1997.

Chapter 7

MRS. CLINTON GOES
TO WASHINGTON

Since her time as First Lady, Hillary Clinton has successfully run two elections and, equally important, has succeeded in office as a senator. Campaigning and governing are two distinct activities, which merit separate
consideration. A successful campaigner does not always excel at the transition into governance upon election, and vice versa. The techniques,
skills, and assets required for one activity do not necessarily translate to
the other. Fortunately for Mrs. Clinton, she appears to excel at both. Her
two Senate campaigns will be discussed first, followed by an analysis of her
first term in office.

FIRST ELECTION

In 2000 Hillary Clinton made history by becoming the junior senator
from New York. While her opponent made much of her non–New Yorker
status, calling her a carpetbagger, the election ultimately was anticlimactic,
with Mrs. Clinton claiming victory with 55 percent of the vote. The First
Lady's campaign for the Senate was one of energizing her strong supporters
(notably African Americans, who turned out in unprecedented numbers—
90 percent of those who voted opted for Mrs. Clinton[1]) and neutralizing
her opponents. Bill Clinton has always been exceptionally popular among
the African American community, and it is likely that much of that support transferred to Mrs. Clinton when she ran for office. Hillary Clinton's
campaign was notable for the support she received not only from African
Americans, but from Democrats generally. The Senate election yielded

one of the largest turnouts among Democrats in the last several decades.[2] Perhaps most importantly, she did not neglect upstate New York, despite the fact that it is overwhelmingly Republican. She put considerable time into the region, campaigning there frequently and hard. It should be noted that Hillary Clinton clearly benefited from a poorly run campaign by her opponent, Rick Lazio. In fairness, he was hurt at the outset by a late start but never changed his message from that of being the true New Yorker in the race. Ultimately, New Yorkers decided that Mrs. Clinton's outsider status was not the hindrance Lazio hoped it would be.

In many respects, Hillary Clinton was the dominant player in the field, and the identity of her opponent was virtually irrelevant; Rick Lazio's approach to the campaign did little to disprove that theory. Rather than discussing issues, he focused solely on the outsider status of his opponent; he avoided his natural base in upstate New York and was oddly aggressive in his interactions with Mrs. Clinton, particularly in their first debate. By focusing more on her than on his own qualifications and the issues, he failed to provide voters with a reason to vote for him. By the end of the campaign, the media "had dubbed Lazio 'Little Ricky' illustrating a perceived lack of stature and presence."[3] In contrast, Hillary Clinton spent 16 months of hard campaigning around the entire state and grudgingly earned the respect of many New Yorkers. Lazio was unable to keep up with her efforts.

In order to better understand the dynamics of the 2000 Senate election, it is important to understand the geography of New York. The division between upstate and downstate New York cannot be overstated. The political culture of the two regions differs vastly and in turn creates tensions for those running in the state, whether Democrat or Republican. Upstate New York has an economy that is largely rural-based and predominantly Republican in voting preferences. There are several major industries located in upstate New York, including Xerox, Corning, and Kodak. In contrast to downstate, upstate New York is mostly white, with little diversity in ethnicity or race. New York City, the locus of downstate New York, tends to vote overwhelmingly Democratic, is the financial capital of the world, and is quite heterogeneous ethnically and racially. The upstate-downstate division often dictates campaign strategies, with upstate New Yorkers deeply critical of downstaters (particularly when it comes to economic issues) and the upstate region having more in common with the Midwest.[4] There is a vast gulf between the two regions of the state, a gulf that crosses cultural and economic lines. Most critically for the 2000 candidates, upstate New York faced greater economic challenges than did downstate New York.

Democrats know that their base supporters come from downstate New York, with its large African American, Latino, Asian, and Jewish populations. Thus turnout is essential for Democratic candidates. If they are able to get voters to the polls, they have the numbers to prevail over most statewide Republican candidates. The number of registered Democrats outweighs the number of registered Republicans by nearly two million people. Thus it is considered a safe Democratic state. Indeed, President Clinton fared extremely well in New York in his two elections. He continues to be extremely popular with New Yorkers, which may help explain his wife's decision to run in the seat vacated by Senator Daniel Patrick Moynihan. Yet, it needs to be remembered that her election was not simply due to her husband's popularity. While New York consistently votes Democratic at the presidential level, New Yorkers have twice elected Republican George Pataki as governor three times and New York City residents elected Republican Rudy Giuliani as mayor two times. Yet Hillary Clinton clearly thought she could benefit from her status as First Lady and as a strong Democrat. While Gore avoided highlighting his linkage to the Clinton administration when running for president in 2000, Mrs. Clinton made it a central point of her campaign.[5]

Hillary Clinton's opponent in the 2000 election, Republican Rick Lazio, entered the campaign late due to the abrupt withdrawal by Mayor Rudy Giuliani. Eleven days after the Republican nominating convention and five months before the general election, Giuliani opted to bow out of the election due to a diagnosis of prostate cancer. Lazio was quickly selected to replace Giuliani. Lazio was an eight-year veteran of the House of Representatives elected from Suffolk County. Lazio was relatively active during his eight years in office and maintained a moderate voting record.[6] On social issues, such as the Brady Bill, family leave, the striker replacement bill, and the assault weapons ban, his votes tended to align with more traditionally Democratic positions.[7] Lazio was a hard worker in Congress and successfully represented his constituents. After eight years in office, it was clear that he had the relevant political experience for running for the Senate.

In contrast, while Hillary Clinton was clearly politically adept and experienced, she did not have a comparable background in legislative politics. Rather, her experience was more as a political activist from her younger days and also came from working on policy proposals such as health care reform. While she is a strong advocate for women and children and has traveled the world arguing for human rights, she did not have any kind of legislative record. Political scientists talk about two kinds of candidates running for office: those who are qualified and those who are not. Qualified candidates tend to be individuals who have previously held elective office (at any level) and have name recognition. What is interesting about the Clinton-Lazio match up is that while Lazio met the previous-experience criteria, he did not have name recognition outside of his own district. In contrast, while Hillary Clinton did not have the previous experience (at least as narrowly measured by equating previous experience with having held elective office), she was off the charts in terms of her name recognition. Arguably, in terms of an election in a state the size of New York, name recognition trumps experience, particularly when the name recognition is international and can generate fundraising at unprecedented levels.

Even prior to Senator Moynihan's retirement from office, there were suggestions that Mrs. Clinton run for office in her own right. Indeed, in October 1998, Representative Charles Rangel (D-NY) from Harlem suggested that Mrs. Clinton consider running in New York. Mrs. Clinton played coy for quite awhile about whether she was interested but eventually launched what she termed a "listening tour"[8] of the state, which culminated in her decision to launch her Senate campaign. Lazio was quickly out of his league running against the First Lady. Any election has its own challenges, but taking on all the trappings that came with Hillary Clinton's position was a virtually insurmountable challenge. Indeed, Lazio could not even benefit from the successful passage of a piece of legislation that he had sponsored. Lazio had sponsored a bill to increase funding for breast cancer treatment for indigent women. Generally, such a bill would merit signature from the president in a Rose Garden ceremony attended by the bill's sponsors. This would allow Lazio to claim credit[9] back home about the kinds of successes he could be expected to continue once in the Senate. However, because the president was also the husband of Lazio's opponent for the Senate, Lazio was denied this ceremony, and President Clinton signed the bill privately, postponing the celebration until after the Senate election.[10]

Money was another source of great disparity between the two candidates. As previously mentioned, Hillary Clinton was able to draw on her White House connections to raise a lot of money. For Hillary's 53rd birthday instead of presenting her with jewelry or some other gift, President Clinton hosted a fundraiser that brought $2 million into her campaign coffers.[11]

Despite the unusual circumstances of having a sitting First Lady running for office, much of the campaign followed the traditional upstate-downstate script. Hillary Clinton worked hard to display her understanding of the special challenges facing upstate New York and devised a plan to address its economic problems. Lazio, in contrast, was considered out of touch and uninterested in upstate New York. In one of the three debates between Lazio and Hillary Clinton, he suggested that upstate New York's economy had "turned the corner" and was improving.[12] Many local residents took issue with Lazio's contention, having felt firsthand the decreasing number of job opportunities and increasing number of layoffs.[13] Toward the end of the campaign, Lazio found himself working extremely hard to win the support of a region that should have been his natural base. Hillary Clinton was able to parlay his ignorance of upstate New York with an ad portraying him as an ostrich with his head in the sand.[14] In contrast, Lazio used the media to try to demonstrate his previous experience in office compared with the outsider status of Hillary Clinton. In addition to the upstate/downstate rivalry, both candidates found themselves, as many before them, courting Jewish voters. Mrs. Clinton and Lazio each worked hard to assure the Jewish population of their support for Israel in order to try to win this key voting bloc.

Lazio's principal approach to fighting Hillary Clinton was labeling her a carpetbagger. Her detractors suggested that selecting New York's seat was quite simply a power play by someone with ambition to ultimately run for president. Her supporters, however, argued that the two states that would have made more sense (Illinois or Arkansas) had no Senate race in 2000; thus New York was an obvious choice, given its open seat and the support its voters had given President Clinton in the two previous elections. Mrs. Clinton only needed to establish residency in New York by the time of election day. Hillary Clinton was not the first candidate to run in New York who was not from New York. In 1964 Robert F. Kennedy successfully ran for the Senate, despite being from a neighboring state.

Hillary Clinton won the election with a 12-point spread (55% to 43%). Everyone was surprised by her victory. While those who were strongly opposed to the First Lady did vote for Lazio, he failed to move any one else to his side. He never managed to provide voters with a positive reason to vote for him and instead focused on discrediting Mrs. Clinton, which was simply not a winning strategy. Those who voted for that very reason would already select Lazio, but those who did not care about Hillary Clinton's outsider status needed a better justification for a Lazio vote—and he simply failed to provide that justification. As a result, those unsure of Mrs. Clinton either opted not to vote or decided to vote for her because she ran a campaign of issues. She provided voters with many reasons to vote for her despite her so-called carpetbagger status. The First Lady was able to win the votes of many who claimed not to like her. Most surprisingly, she won upstate New York, albeit with a much slimmer margin (50% to 49%). For Lazio to fail in this region starkly highlights the ineffectiveness of his campaign. Upstate New York continues to be Republican territory, with 9 of 13 House elections going to their party. However, as Hillary Clinton demonstrated with her success, upstate New York cannot be taken for granted as Republican territory, at least for state-wide offices. She best summarized the experience and her success: "Sixty-two counties, sixteen months, three debates, two opponents, and six black pantsuits later—here we are!"[15]

REELECTION

In contrast to her election in 2000, in which Hillary Clinton seemed to be constantly front and center in media coverage, the 2006 election was virtually a nonevent. Her opponent, John Spencer, former mayor of Yonkers, spent only $5 million compared with Hillary Clinton's $36 million—together making the New York Senate race the most expensive in the country.[16] It is intriguing that Hillary Clinton would spend so much money, given that she had so little true competition from Spencer. Indeed, she won with 67 percent of the vote. She donated money to other Democratic House races[17] and traveled throughout the state. While money spent in this manner is not surprising, her decisions to spend $13,000 on flowers for fundraisers or thank-yous to donors and $27,000 on valet parking[18] is more surprising than the $17 million spent on advertising. These expenses took a toll on her total war chest (the term used for money raised during a campaign that can be spent on future campaigns), eliminating what could have been a substantial advantage in early money for the expected presidential bid. Nevertheless, Senator Clinton did have the luxury of being able to virtually ignore her opponent and instead talk about national issues or campaign on behalf of others.[19] The *New York Times* endorsed Mrs. Clinton's candidacy and even went so far as to say: "It's a measure of the haplessness of Mr. Spencer's campaign that the Republican nominee has been dogged by rumors that his real aim is to prepare the ground for an attempt to regain his old job as mayor of Yonkers."[20] The endorsement went on to say that Senator Clinton had mastered the issues facing New York and had managed to find a way to work with Republicans once in office. The editorial argued that Mrs. Clinton had finally found her true calling as senator.[21]

The Republicans simply failed to put up a strong challenger for Mrs. Clinton. Perhaps the most media coverage that John Spencer managed to obtain was for his comment that "Mrs. Clinton had evolved from an ugly duckling to the presentable 59-year-old woman she is today with the help of 'millions of dollars' of 'work.'"[22] This was hardly an issue relevant for selecting a senator and was quickly challenged for its sexist overtones. It should not be viewed as particularly surprising that the Republicans were unable to nominate a stronger opponent for Hillary Clinton. In congressional elections, incumbency remains one of the single most important factors when running for office. The most difficult campaign for most representatives and senators is the first one; after that, most members of Congress can feel fairly secure in the likelihood of their reelection. Senator Clinton had name recognition that John Spencer simply did not. Most New Yorkers were unaware of who she was running against. The 2006 election was quite similar to that of the 2004 election when Senator Chuck Schumer ran against a virtually unknown Republican, Howard Mills. Schumer's successful reelection was equally uneventful. The Republican National Party makes strategic decisions about which elections are worth investing in; taking on a popular incumbent like Chuck Schumer or Hillary Clinton is not a good investment. Money could be better spent on races where there is a greater chance of the Republican candidate prevailing. As a consequence, John Spencer and Howard Mills could not rely on their own national party for much support since its resources would be better placed elsewhere.

The question that must be addressed then is why Hillary Clinton spent so much money on her campaign. The race was never competitive. John Spencer was unlikely to ever mount a true offensive against her, yet she spent more money than any other candidate running for the Senate. Most suggest that she did so to lay the groundwork for a presidential bid. The focus of the campaign against her was less about her abilities as a senator and more about the likelihood of her making a run for the presidency in 2008.

IN OFFICE

Switching the focus from campaign activities to governance, it becomes clear that Hillary Clinton understood how to make the transition successfully. Pundits initially expected Senator Clinton to enter office and look for opportunities to steal the limelight. After all she had spent eight years as First Lady, taking a much more active role than most who came before her (and after as it turns out). Moreover, she had previously established relationships, some quite contentious, with senators already in office. She had worked with members of Congress while pursuing her changes to health care policy. Yet, despite the baggage of the past with which she arrived in the Senate, she surprised nearly everyone. Hillary

Clinton implicitly seemed to understand the need to be a junior senator in the same mold as any other newly elected official. She attended the so-called transition classes for new members of Congress and learned the ropes along with other members of her electoral cohort. Other than entering the Senate with a security detail, Senator Clinton was like most other new members. She did not seek the limelight and would often let Senator Schumer, the senior member from New York, take the initiative on legislation focused on the state.

Senator Clinton defied the very expectations that much of the public and, most importantly, her former enemies had of her. While she made the transition seem relatively easy, it is important to note that her success stemmed from her previous failures while First Lady. In particular, her efforts on behalf of transforming the health care system ultimately paid dividends for her when she least expected it: upon becoming a senator herself. At the time when she was pursuing her legislative goals, many of her opponents did not question her policy expertise but did criticize her failure to understand the politics of the situation. In short, she could hold her own while testifying in a committee hearing, but she was unable to understand the politics of the cloakroom and how to work the system and work with those she needed in Congress.[23] She was determined not to repeat the same mistakes once she became a member of the very institution that so challenged her in the past.

One of the key tactics that Mrs. Clinton took upon entering the Senate was to curry the favor of Senator Robert Byrd, the very same individual who virtually single-handedly ensured the failure of her health care proposal several years previously. Byrd assumed that the new senator would presume upon her former title of First Lady and expect special consideration, but he eventually became one of her greatest champions. Senator Clinton recognized the need to learn more about the institution, and upon winning her election, she asked Senator Byrd to teach her how to be a model senator.[24] According to Joshua Green, author of an article in the *Atlantic Monthly*, Hillary Clinton's meeting with Byrd sent a public signal that she did not plan on showboating when in Congress and also a private signal to Byrd that she wanted to apprentice under him. Moreover, she went so far as to arrange for Senator Byrd to conduct regular parliamentarian workshops for a group of newly elected senators.[25] Her time with Byrd ultimately paid substantial dividends for her when New York was most in need of assistance. After the September 11 attacks on the World Trade Center, Senator Clinton contacted Senator Byrd, who was chair of the Appropriations Committee, to ask for financial assistance for the city. She received the help and was able to secure $20 billion for recovery—clearly an important legislative outcome for the new senator.[26]

In addition to courting Senator Byrd, Mrs. Clinton indicated her desire to be treated no differently from her other new colleagues in yet another manner. In a city where most people work to be in the public spotlight, Senator Clinton usually steps back during photo opportunities. She is even willing to get coffee for her colleagues, thereby further defying their expectations of a militant feminist.[27] However, despite her attempts to appear nonthreatening to her colleagues and dispel her liberal stereotype, she quietly bucked the system in her own way. Congress remains a very traditional institution with the expectation that women will wear appropriate clothing, meaning skirts or dresses. Indeed, until he was forced to resign from office, Senator Trent Lott preferred a so-called lipstick-and-skirt dress code. Women are still expected to cover their blouses when on the floor of the Senate and make sure that their shoulders are not bare. For her own quiet rebellion, predominantly demonstrated by wearing pantsuits, Senator Clinton is liked by female staff members from both parties. One staffer pointed in particular to the fact that she wore a pant-suit for her swearing in ceremony—something not typically done by newly elected senators—as evidence of the ways in which Mrs. Clinton pushes back against the prevailing system.[28]

Ironically, there were some cries that Senator Clinton was too quiet and meek during her initial time in office.[29] Many expected her behavior to be similar to what she exhibited as the wife of President Clinton, facing off with anyone bent on destroying her husband's career. However, that was not to be the case in the beginning of her tenure in the Senate. There were some suggestions that her timidity was a function of the investigation into last-minute pardons issued by President Clinton before leaving the Oval Office.[30] However, she was taking her time to learn the mores and norms of the office, as most newly elected members do.[31] It is noteworthy that in a LexisNexis search on articles about Hillary Clinton's first year as senator, only 76 articles appeared in the Washington, D.C., papers, and of those, only a few are actually about her time in office. Others discuss the pardons offered by her husband, the clothes she wore while taking the oath of office, and the office space she rented in Manhattan. Senator Clinton did not make much substantive news as a senator during her first year in office. It should be noted that few newly elected senators hit the ground running and make a splash in the legislative arena. Rather, they need time to complete a successful transition to learn the rules of the institution. While Mrs. Clinton may have had knowledge of the Senate that was different from other newly elected senators due to her former role as First Lady, she still had much to learn. And like other newly elected senators, she took this need seriously.

Not surprisingly, Senator Clinton received more attention from the New York papers in this same period. However, many of the articles focused on scandals involving her husband (the pardons), her brother, and her acceptance of gifts that were considered to be excessive and unethical. Relatively few of the stories involved her actions as a senator, demonstrating the extent to which she did remain in the background once in office. This was not to be the case throughout her entire first term in office, however, nor would that have been considered a desirable approach for any senator to take. While there is some expectation that newly arrived senators will learn from their elders, the norm of remaining in the background does not last as long as it once did. Today we expect all of our representatives to work on our behalf. Once the learning curve kicks in, junior senators are expected to begin working and making a difference. Senator Clinton was able to do just that.

She began her time in office with appointments to three committees: Armed Services, Environment and Public Works, and Health, Education, Labor and Pensions. She also sits on the Senate Special Committee on Aging. Although she desired a seat on the powerful Appropriations Committee (which makes decisions about allocation of spending), rarely is such an assignment given to a junior senator. Hillary Clinton was no exception and had to make do with assignments to her backup selections.[32] In addition to her committee assignments, she sits on a variety of subcommittees within each committee. The assignment to Health, Education, Labor, and Pensions fits quite well with her longstanding commitment to women's and children's issues, and she has continued to work toward pursuing their improvement.

Political scientists talk about so-called homestyle[33] when they consider the behavior of members in their home constituency. For Senator Clinton, this would be the entire state of New York. Regardless of her junior status as senator for the state, she is still expected to serve her constituents, as well as the nation more generally. Toward that end, she opened up nine offices outside of Washington, which are spread around the state. The office she procured in Manhattan caused some comment due to its cost of over $500,000/month. Her colleague, Senator Chuck Schumer, pays closer to $200,000/month. Yet it is entirely at the discretion of each individual senator how to allocate the funding they receive for maintaining their offices. In the Internet age, it has become a very simple matter to communicate information to constituents. They only need access Senator Clinton's Web page (http://clinton.senate.gov/index.cfm) to find a host of information about her offices, constituent services, and activities within government.

One of the main activities for all members of Congress is writing bills. Senator Clinton focused her first pieces of legislation on assisting the upstate New York economy.[34] By her first 100-day mark, she was receiving solid reviews: "Clinton has emerged as a blend of celebrity—gawked at by Capitol Hill tourists and pursued by reporters—and workhorse, who has near perfect attendance at committee hearings and digs into policy minutiae with gusto."[35] By this measuring stick, she had already sponsored 20 bills and amendments, a number that greatly exceeds most of the newly elected senators.[36] By the end of her first year in office, she had cosponsored 316 bills, resolutions, and amendments. This is an important activity for Mrs. Clinton since it provides her with the means for taking positions on pieces of legislation that might be important to New Yorkers. While she still remained true to her longstanding interest in health care and children's issues, she appropriately incorporated more local issues into her agenda as well.

In her first year in office, Senator Clinton introduced 31 different public bills, of which 3 were Senate resolutions (meaning that they are nonbinding and are rarely controversial). Senator Clinton's bills were referred to several different committees, including Finance, Health Education and Labor, Banking, Environment and Judiciary. The topic of the legislation usually dictates where the bill will be sent since each committee has its own content jurisdiction, ensuring that sponsored bills will be sent to the appropriate location. While there are advantages to sending legislation to one's own committee—thereby increasing the odds of it receiving some time in deliberation, at least at the committee level—this cannot always be done. Of the 31 pieces of legislation that Hillary Clinton introduced, 2 became public laws. The first, S. 584, allowed for a U.S. courthouse in New York to be renamed the "Thurgood Marshall United States Courthouse." While this is hardly life-altering legislation, it should be noted that it nevertheless took five months to complete the process. The bill was first introduced March 21, 2001, and was signed into public law on August 20, 2001. The second bill to be made into law was S. 1622, which was designed to provide unemployment assistance to victims of 9/11. This legislation had more far-reaching impact than the first bill for which Hillary Clinton can claim credit; however, it was also unlikely to produce much controversy given the subject. It bears noting that 2 out of 31 bills is a success rate very much in line with the overall rate of approximately 10 percent of all introduced bills becoming law.

Senator Clinton hit the ground running after her decisive reelection to the Senate. She immediately pursued her legislative agenda, sponsoring 53 separate pieces of legislation. It is important to note that among the 53 pieces of legislation, there are amendments and Senate resolutions; nevertheless, she clearly continues her active role as a legislator. All bills are certainly not created equal, and Senate resolutions are generally not considered to be of the same magnitude of importance as Senate bills. For example, on March 1, 2007, Mrs. Clinton introduced S. Con. Res. 10, "Honoring and praising the National Association for the Advancement of Colored People on the occasion of its 98th anniversary." It is difficult to imagine such a piece of legislation sparking controversy, regardless of party.

Pulling the lens of analysis back, we can examine data from Mrs. Clinton's entire time spent in the Senate. Since her first day in office, she has sponsored a total of 285 bills, of which only 40 have made it out of committee and 2 have become law.[37] While this number seems incredibly small, it should be noted that it is not an atypical number, particularly the final passage statistic, for any senator. With two bills enacted, Hillary Clinton is average in her success rate compared with her peers.[38] In addition to sponsoring her own legislation, in the same time period (essentially the entire time that she has been in office to date), she has cosponsored 1,478 bills, again a level of activity that is average compared with her colleagues. Voting is another critical activity of legislators. Missing votes is generally frowned upon by constituents and can become a factor in reelection. Indeed, in New York's 1998 Senate election, both candidates, D'Amato and Schumer, traded barbs about their respective attendance records. Hillary Clinton, however, is unlikely to have her own record used against her; she has missed only 43 out of 2,080, or 2 percent, of votes since January 23, 2001.[39]

Another measure of a member's legislative activities is his or her interest-group ratings. All interest groups identify legislation that they consider essential to their mission and analyze the extent to which a member votes in line with the interest group's preferences. These measures become useful proxies for evaluating the liberalness or conservativeness of individual legislators. They also provide summary information about the voting history of the members of Congress. Interest-group ratings can be used by academics, voters, other interest groups, and other members of Congress to obtain information about the legislative priorities and beliefs of legislators. When members of Congress vote, they use a variety of different cues[40] to help them decide how to vote. These cues include constituents, interest groups, fellow members of Congress, party leadership, and, of course, the member's own beliefs and preferences. When issues are salient to the district, members will need to take those preferences into consideration. For those issues that are below the radar of constituents, members of Congress tend to look elsewhere for information, especially on issues that are not necessarily their own top priority. Party leaders will also attempt to influence legislators, particularly on issues that are critical to the party mission. However, party discipline is notoriously weak in the U.S. Congress, and party leaders have few sanctions at their disposal to enforce party unity. Interest groups also provide information for members; the provision of a rating system can prove useful in such circumstances. Senator Clinton has fairly traditional liberal ratings on most groups. Project Vote Smart (http://www.votesmart.org) provides an extensive record of Hillary Clinton's voting record by numerous issues ranging from abortion to education to budget and environmental issues.

Two of the more common interest groups that provide ratings of interest to scholars are the Chamber of Commerce, representing business issues, and the American Civil Liberties Union (ACLU), representing civil rights and liberties. For the Chamber of Commerce, Senator Clinton has ranged from 35 to 50 percent, indicating that over her time in office her votes have aligned with the interests of the Chamber 35 to 50 percent. The Chamber of Commerce rating is generally used as a proxy for conservatism. Senator Clinton's rating indicates that she is more liberal than conservative, but it should be kept in mind that there are plenty of representatives in office with a rating of 0 percent. In contrast, Senator Clinton has ranged from a low of 60 percent voting with the interests of the ACLU in 2001–2002 to a high of 83 percent in 2005–2006. In many ways, the ACLU and the Chamber of Commerce should be expected to be the inverse of one another since the ACLU is frequently the proxy used to measure liberalism. This seems to be the case for Senator Clinton. She is more comfortable voting with the ACLU's preferred positions than those of the Chamber of Commerce. According to the *National Journal*, Hillary Clinton is one of the most conservative Democrats on foreign policy; only 5 other Democrats received more conservative rankings than she did.[41]

Hardly surprising, Senator Clinton continues her efforts to reform health care. While her approach may differ significantly from her attempts while First Lady, she has used her position in the Senate to try to come up with new methods for improving health care provision. One approach in particular that she has taken is to focus on the bureaucracy of health care. She argues that doctors spend too much time on paperwork when they could instead be allocating more time to their patients.

In addition to the sheer amount of time spent on paperwork, much of that paperwork is redundant and costly. Her legislation aims to improve that situation[42] through the usage of electronic medical records (EMRs). What is significant about this legislative approach is the extent to which it can cross party lines. It is a prime example of Senator Clinton's newly found technique of working with Republicans in the Senate to accomplish her goals. Indeed, reforming health care by incorporating advances in technology is no doubt more politically palatable than the health care plan that she worked so hard on while First Lady. More recently, Mrs. Clinton has resumed her calls for universal health coverage but has yet to provide the details of how this goal would be achieved.

The most current legislation that she has introduced includes S. 820, "Choice in Child Care Act" (referred to the Health Committee), which would provide demonstration projects for at-home infant care for low-income families. Between five and seven states would receive a grant to participate in the program. Senator Clinton introduced the same legislation in the previous session, but it never went beyond the committee referral.[43] Such is the game of politics. Many more bills are introduced than are ever reported out of committee. If nothing happens before the end of the session, the senator must reintroduce the legislation in the subsequent session. A new piece of legislation (not introduced in a previous congressional session) is S. 837, "I LEAD Act of 2007" (also referred to the Health Committee). The goal of this legislation is considerably broader in scope: it strives to "develop a generation of school leaders who are committed to, and effective in, increasing student achievement and to ensure that all low-income, under-performing schools are led by effective school leaders who are well-prepared to foster student success."[44] The mechanism for achieving this goal is to recruit and train principals to help foster leadership and management skills.[45]

One of the more interesting hallmarks of Senator Clinton's first term in office has been the extent to which she has been willing (and even instrumental) to establish bipartisan opportunities for writing legislation. One of the forums that has permitted her the opportunity to not only debunk some of the preconceived notions about who she is but to forge cross-party alliances is the congressional prayer group, Fellowship. Fellowship dates back to the 1930s, with regular breakfast meetings having been held since 1943.[46] Today it continues to hold weekly meetings and is one of the few remaining venues where partisanship is put aside. Each meeting begins with one of the attendees giving personal testimony. At one such moment, Senator Sam Brownback, a conservative who was planning on talking about a personal health issue instead stopped when he saw Hillary

Clinton in attendance. He had never been one of her supporters or admirers, but at that moment, he asked her forgiveness and offered her an apology for his past actions pertaining to her, which she accepted.[47] While this is certainly a nice story, it has significant political implications as well. Hillary Clinton has always been a devout Christian. Joining the prayer group was entirely in character for her in terms of the centrality that religion plays in her life. She then used that activity as an opportunity to join with members of the prayer group on legislative endeavors, regardless of individuals' party affiliations. Senator Clinton ended up working with Senator Brownback to cosponsor legislation to protect refugees running from sexual abuse and a second bill to study whether children are harmed by violence in video games and on television.[48]

Brownback is not the only member of the prayer group that Senator Clinton has teamed up with. Working with staunchly conservative colleagues has substantially helped Mrs. Clinton to moderate her liberal image and has provided her with a broader base of appeal for her legislative activities. And these same pairings may later prove beneficial in her presidential bid. It should be noted that she is not alone in benefiting from the bipartisan pairings. Indeed, some of her very conservative colleagues have also received similar advantages from working with her—namely, moderating their more conservative reputations. Thus, Rick Santorum, Newt Gingrich, and Bill Frist were all the beneficiaries of Hillary Clinton's more moderating presence, just as they assisted in softening her liberal reputation.[49]

Perhaps one of the unique ways in which Senator Clinton has parlayed her former role as First Lady is her ability to call meetings and bring together different players to forge partnerships to assist her constituency. When her legislation, like almost all sponsored bills, ended up stuck in committee, Senator Clinton took a different approach to try to provide economic benefits to New York. This was particularly the case for her efforts to create more jobs upstate. When campaigning for her first term, she promised to create 200,000 new jobs. Upon realization that any legislation she proposed to fulfill her promise would be unlikely to get out of committee, she instead embarked on a venture capitalism project sponsored by New Jobs for New York (NJNY). Senator Clinton created NJNY, which combines "private enterprise and government largesse, big-money insider connections and wonky policy notions,"[50] to secure her goal of helping New York.

By most measures, Hillary Clinton has been a very successful senator. As of late 2006, Senator Clinton was enjoying an approval rating of 74 percent—a full 18 points higher than the average approval rating for senators.[51] Moreover, she is fulfilling Mayhew's predictions about what we should expect from our legislators: advertising, credit claiming, and position taking.[52] New Yorkers regularly receive information from her office about activities on their behalf (advertising), she takes credit for the bills that she sponsors or cosponsors that succeed (credit claiming), and she regularly presents her positions on the issues of the day (position taking). She is a powerful voice on national issues, particularly in opposition to the Iraq War. While she did initially vote for the resolution supporting President Bush's actions, in recent months, she has become increasingly vocal against the American presence in Iraq. After a recent tour of Iraq, Afghanistan, and Pakistan, Senator Clinton returned to the United States opposing President Bush's decision to increase the number of troops being sent to war in what became labeled a surge. Most recently, as she has begun touring for her presidential campaign, she has argued ever more forcibly against the war in Iraq. Senator Clinton has even gone so far as to say that—while she stands behind her vote based on the information she had available at the time—if she knew then what she knows today, she would have voted differently.

From this point on it will become increasingly difficult to differentiate between Hillary Clinton's activities as senator and those geared toward her presidential campaign. Almost anything she does now will be framed within the context of the 2008 election. Her days as a back bencher are long over, and now everyone will be watching her closely, not just New Yorkers. However, just like all of the other senators running for president, Senator Clinton will need to find the balance between the demands of running for president and maintaining the trust of her current constituents and fulfilling her obligation to them as their junior senator. While this is no easy task, it certainly seems well within the capabilities of Mrs. Clinton.

NOTES

    1. Paul H. Johnson, "Blacks Plan to Watch the Winners They Backed," *Record*, November 9, 2000.

    2. Fred Kaplan, "Election 2000: Clinton Wins Seat in Senate," *Boston Globe*, November 8, 2000.

    3. Dena Levy and Charles Tien, "Clinton Defeats Lazio in New York's Senate Race," in *The Roads to Congress*, ed. Sunil Ahuja and Robert Dewhirst (New York: Wadsworth, 2002), p. 149.

    4. Ibid., p. 151.

    5. Ibid.

6. Ibid.

7. Ibid., p. 153.

8. Beth J. Harpaz, *The Girl's in the Van: A Reporter's Diary of the Campaign Trail* (New York: Thomas Dunne Books, 2001).

9. David R. Mayhew, *Congress: The Electoral Connection* (New Haven, Conn.: Yale University Press, 1974).

10. Dena Levy and Charles Tien, "Clinton Defeats Lazio in New York's Senate Race," in *The Roads to Congress*, ed. Sunil Ahuja and Robert Dewhirst (New York: Wadsworth, 2002).

11. Ibid.

12. Ibid.

13. Lara Jakes, "Clinton Targets Upstate Recovery," *Times Union*, November 9, 2000.

14. Ibid.

15. Ibid., p. 162.

16. *New York Times*, "Most Expensive Races of 2006," November 14, 2006.

17. Marc Santora, "Clinton Gains Second Term Easily, with Support Extending across Much of the State," *New York Times*, November 8, 2006.

18. Anne E. Kornblut and Jeff Zeleny, "Clinton Won Easily, but Bankroll Shows the Toll," *New York Times*, November 21, 2006.

19. Marc Santora, "A Gap Never Closed," *New York Times*, November 7, 2006.

20. "The New York Senate Race," editorial, *New York Times*, October 15, 2006.

21. Ibid.

22. Marc Sanotra, "Who Cares About the Issues: Is That Botox," *New York Times*, October 26, 2006.

23. Joshua Green, "Take Two: How Hillary Clinton Turned Herself into the Consummate Washington Player," *Atlantic Monthly*, November 2006.

24. Ibid.

25. Ibid.

26. Ibid.

27. Chris Smith, "The Woman in the Bubble: After Years of Public Trauma, Hillary Clinton Is Secure, Triumphant, Joyous Even. Is it Worth Giving Up All That for the White House?" *New York Magazine*, November 13, 2006, pp. 30–39.

28. Joshua Green, "Take Two: How Hillary Clinton Turned Herself into the Consummate Washington Player," *Atlantic Monthly*, November 2006.

29. Dick Morris, "Is Hillary Frightened," *The Hill*, May 2, 2001.

30. Ibid.

31. Donald R. Matthews, *U.S. Senators and Their World* (Westport, Conn.: Greenwood Press, 1980).

32. Timothy J. Burger, "Health Panel Seen for Hil," *Daily News* (New York), January 11, 2001.

33. Richard F. Fenno, Jr. *Home Style: House Members in Their Districts*" (Boston: Little, Brown and Company, 1978).

34. Vincent Morris, "Hill's New Bills Would Boost N.Y.," *New York Post,* March 2, 2001.

35. Shannon McCaffrey, "Hillary Clinton's First 100 Days: Small Victories for a Big Celebrity," *Associated Press,* April 11, 2001.

36. Ibid.

37. GovTrack.us. http://www.govtrack.us/congress/person.xpd?id=300022.

38. Ibid.

39. Ibid.

40. John W. Kingdon, "Models of Legislative Voting," *Journal of Politics* (August 1977): 563–95.

41. Matt Bai, "Mrs. Triangulation," *New York Times Magazine,* October 2, 2005.

42. Erik L. Goldman, "Sen. Clinton Eyes EMRs as New Key to Reform: 10 Years Later," *Family Practice News* 34, no. 6 (March 15, 2004): 4–6.

43. GovTrack.us. http://www.govtrack.us/congress/bill.xpd?bill=s110–820.

44. GovTrack.us. http://www.govtrack.us/congress/billtext.xpd?bill=s110–837.

45. Ibid.

46. Joshua Green, "Take Two: How Hillary Clinton Turned Herself into the Consummate Washington Player," *Atlantic Monthly,* November 2006.

47. Ibid.

48. Ibid.

49. Ibid.

50. Chris Smith, "The Woman in the Bubble: After Years of Public Trauma, Hillary Clinton Is Secure, Triumphant, Joyous Even. Is it Worth Giving Up All That for the White House?" *New York Magazine,* November 13, 2006, pp. 30–39.

51. GovTrack.us. http://www.govtrack.us/congress/person.xpd?id=300022.

52. David R. Mayhew, *Congress: The Electoral Connection* (New Haven, Conn.: Yale University Press, 1974).

Chapter 8

PRESIDENTIAL CAMPAIGN

What is Hillary Rodham Clinton's future? She has come a long way from the studious child from Park Ridge. Hillary Clinton has the opportunity to make history and finally live out her own ambitions, putting her career first and allowing her husband to continue in the supporting role that he has occupied since 2000 when Mrs. Clinton entered the Senate. The 2008 presidential race is already noteworthy for beginning earlier than any other presidential election. Traditionally, candidates do not declare their intent to run for office until the fall before the actual election. In a break from the norm, candidates began announcing in early 2007. Senator Hillary Clinton effectively threw down the gauntlet by announcing her intention to run for president on January 20, 2007, almost two full years before the general election. Her close competitor, Senator Barack Obama, joined the fray by announcing his plans to run for office on February 10, 2007.

Hillary Clinton is not the first woman to run for president. Over 20 women have run for the office, 15 of whom were running for one of the major political parties.[1] However, none made it through the primary, and many even dropped out before the party nominating conventions. Most recently, in 2004, Carol Mosley Braun was among the Democratic candidates seeking the nomination, and in 2000, Elizabeth Dole ran for president. However, Dole was forced to drop out before the end of the primary season due to an inability to raise sufficient funds in the face of then Governor George Bush's dominance among the Republican candidates. The first woman to make it onto the general ballot for high office was

Geraldine Ferraro, running as the vice presidential candidate with Walter Mondale in 1984.

Polling results provide encouragement for those interested in seeing a woman elected to the highest office in the country. A *Newsweek* poll taken in December 2006 found that 86 percent of respondents claimed that they would vote for a qualified woman if nominated by their party.[2] Of course, it should be noted that there can be some error in these results. While scientific polling certainly provides useful snapshots of what the American public is thinking, respondents are aware that some views are not ones to state publicly. For example, saying that women are not capable of being president is not politically correct; thus the results may be an inflation of the number of people Americans who are truly willing to vote for a woman as president. The only way to ultimately determine that number is by having a woman on the ballot.

There are numerous explanations offered for the relative paucity of women in politics in the United States. While women make strides in many other arenas, they continue to lag behind most other nations when it comes to elected office, particularly at the executive level where there has never been a woman president. Explanations generally differentiate between either systemic reasons or psychological reasons. Systemic explanations focus on the structure of the congressional system, where each seat reflects a single-member plurality district (SMPD). That is, the individual with the plurality of the vote wins the entire seat. Women need to actually run in the seats to be elected to them. This is in contrast to a proportional system where parties put up a slate of candidates to fill the proportion of the vote they receive in the election. In this system, the party has considerably more latitude to get women into office by including them on the slate of candidates. In the SMPD system, it is largely up to the women to self-select themselves to run for office. If they do not get their names on the ballot, they have no opportunity to be elected. Of course, women in the proportional system have to indicate their interest in being elected, but they do not have to run individually in the same manner as in the United States, where elections are candidate-centered.

Support for the systemic explanation can be found in the incumbency rate of women. Once they have successfully negotiated their first election, they are just as likely to return to office as their male colleagues. However, that first election is the difficult one. New candidates for office, whether males or females, fare better when they run in seats without an incumbent. However, with reelection rates over 90 percent in the House, open seats are not very plentiful. As a result, women are not elected, and the pool of qualified female candidates for even higher office, such as the presidency, is small. Another factor may be that women, for whatever reason, opt out of running for office. This could be due to the tendency for women still to assume the primary responsibility for child care and the need to wait to run for office until their children are older. This again shrinks the pool of potential women to enter politics.

Alternative explanations lie with the voters. There are suggestions that Americans are simply not comfortable voting for women. This outlook suggests that the world of politics is best left to men and that women are not ready to tackle difficult policy problems such as foreign policy. However, the fact that women have the same incumbency rates as men belies this explanation. Or, perhaps once a woman has been elected, her gender no longer seems as relevant as her track record in office. Certainly Hillary Clinton had a very different experience in her two elections for the Senate. In the first, there was considerable coverage of her hairstyle and her choice of clothing (typically black pantsuits with pink sweaters thrown over her shoulders). In the second election, her outfits were not discussed, and only her opponent commented about her physical appearance when suggesting that she had plastic surgery. Male colleagues rarely receive attention for their appearance, unless some aspect of it becomes symbolic of the campaign itself. Such was the case when Lamar Alexander ran in the 1996 Republican primary wearing a black-and-red plaid shirt in order to convey the image of being a regular person. Similarly, Senator Webb from Virginia wore his son's combat boots throughout the 2006 campaign—this was noteworthy because it became a physical symbol of Webb's opposition to the Iraq War.

It is likely that the lack of women in office is a consequence of both systemic and psychological explanations. There remain individuals who are not comfortable with women in power. Indeed, the recent *Newsweek* poll mentioned earlier in this chapter found that 14 percent of respondents said they would not vote for a woman, even if she were qualified. Likewise, the structure of the political system does not allow a political party to determine that more women need to be in office and then simply make that happen by including more women on the party's slate.

Hillary Clinton seems on the verge of being the first woman who can make the leap to being a serious presidential candidate. On January 20, 2007, she put an end to the years of speculation and formally announced her plans to enter the 2008 presidential race. Many seem to consider her the front-runner for the Democratic nomination, despite the recent popularity of Senator Barack Obama, also running for the Democratic nomination. In addition, six others have also entered the political fray, and while Hillary Clinton has made believers of many New Yorkers, she still needs to persuade millions of other voters across the country of her bona fides to run for office.

Hillary Clinton's presidential campaign will no doubt be an interesting one to watch. In her Senate races, she was very deliberative, especially in the first one when she embarked on her listening tour in order to better understand the dynamics of New York State issues. One can speculate that she will pursue a similar process in the national election; however, it may be too costly, particularly in terms of time. She has the benefits of her national office, but so do many of the other candidates.

Perhaps the greatest obstacle to Hillary's campaign is the extent to which Americans already think they know her. There are few voters who do not already have an opinion formed about her, whether positive or negative. Her detractors find her to be almost too deliberative, too methodical in her decision-making process.[3] However, this has long been her trademark. While many of her fellow nominees ran for the microphone immediately after President Bush announced his plans to increase the number of troops being sent to Iraq, Mrs. Clinton instead took a trip to Iraq, Afghanistan, and Pakistan to receive the most current information possible on the situation in Iraq. It was only upon her return that she made public her position to place a cap on the number of Americans being sent to Iraq.[4] Senator Clinton is under considerable pressure to denounce her 2002 vote in favor of the resolution to support President Bush in his intentions to go to war with Iraq. This pressure is no doubt from the more activist wing of the Democratic Party, which tends to be more liberal than the public at large. In this instance, the more liberal position is to be against the Iraq War. However, among the Democratic candidates, Senator Clinton is the most conservative when it comes to national defense. Her more conservative position relative to her fellow Democratic candidates is not simply artifice. According to the late political columnist, Molly Ivins, Hillary Clinton is "Republican-lite."[5]

Indeed, even before she was elected senator in 2000, she gave a speech stating that the United States must be prepared to not only take on the simple engagements that are clearly winnable, but be willing to take on more difficult situations if the cause is right.[6] This position provides insight into how Hillary Clinton decided to support President Bush in 2002 when faced with the vote for using force against Iraq. It is important to note, however, that Senator Clinton is the only one among the candidates running for office who has had firsthand experience with the demands placed on a president when conducting foreign relations; she saw the difficulties faced by her husband when Congress tried to micromanage his foreign policy plans.[7] While many assume that Hillary Clinton would be reluctant to use force, there is considerable evidence that she holds the military in considerable esteem—remember her attempt to enlist with the Marines.[8] However, she was turned away because of her poor vision and also because she is a woman. This is a story that seems to have received very little play in the media, yet it provides a different perspective on what many presume about Senator Clinton and the military. More recently, she broke with her party by voting to expand the Army, refusing to support a total ban on land mines, and agreeing to support missile defense spending.[9] In many ways, Mrs. Clinton is more comfortable with the Pentagon brass than many of her colleagues, due in large part to her upbringing, which joined together a strong sense of right and wrong with a moral conservatism.[10] This background makes her comfortable with authority, although she is not authoritarian and has great respect for the military.

Mrs. Clinton's vote on Iraq continues to be one that she struggles to explain. And that vote and her need to position herself among the more liberal (antiwar) wing of the Democratic Party in order to win the nomination places pressure on any decision she makes regarding the Iraq War. Indeed, in this instance, it would no doubt be simpler to not be in the Senate when running for president. After the 2006 elections when the House and Senate returned to a Democratic majority, there has been considerable pressure placed on Congress to try to do something to change the direction of the war. This has taken the form of placing conditions on funding of the war. President Bush has declared quite strongly that he will veto any legislation that places limits on the troops, and thus far he has carried out his threats. However, as the deadline for refinancing the war continues, the House and Senate struggle with how to force President Bush's hand. And this in turn places considerable pressure on all candidates running for president who are also in the Senate. Presidential electoral politics are now having a direct impact on how the debate takes shape in the Senate. Both Senator Obama and Senator Clinton have avoided supporting any specific ending date for the war until Senator Dodd, a second-tier presidential candidate, started running ads highlighting the failure of some of his fellow candidates to take a position on the issue. In response, both Obama and Clinton reversed their policies and began arguing for a March 2008 end date.

The Iraq War will no doubt continue to be one of the key issues of the 2008 presidential election, but it is clearly an issue that cuts across party lines and forces both Democratic and Republican candidates to attempt to differentiate themselves from President Bush. Interestingly, in some respects this is more troublesome for the Republican candidates. While Senator Clinton may struggle with her initial vote in favor of the war resolution, she can now say that she is opposed to the continuation of troops in Iraq. Things are not so simple for the Republican candidates who need to balance their own preferences with the need to support President Bush. While the more activist Republican voters (who are the ones to turn out during the nominating season) may continue to support the war effort, the more moderate voters who will come out in the general election may not be so sanguine with such a position. The Republican candidates must figure out a message that will work with both sets of voters.

One of the more interesting challenges facing Senator Clinton, as well as the other nominees, is the ability to raise sufficient funds for the campaign. Hillary Clinton certainly has the advantage of having her husband, Bill Clinton, to help. Senator Clinton's decision to not accept public money for either the primaries or general elections makes the money that she raises independently even more critical. But there are concerns of donor fatigue after the Clintons combined long run in politics[11]—going after the same base of women and African Americans. This concern has materialized as a reality. The 2007 first-quarter financial reports for the presidential candidates indicate that Mrs. Clinton is ahead in money raised for her campaign, but only by $1 million over Senator Barack Obama. Senator Clinton has raised $26 million to his $25 million. Perhaps even more importantly, Obama has twice the number of contributors as Clinton, and of the 100,000 people who have given to his campaign, few have come close to reaching the primary campaign contribution limit. This will allow Senator Obama to return to his contributor base time and again without fear of maxing out their donations. Hillary Clinton's decision to forgo public funding impacts the other candidates; they now have pressure to also forgo public funding so that they can raise and spend at similar levels as Senator Clinton. Thus far, only Senator Obama is able to keep up the pace. Former Senator Edwards is further behind than the other two front runners, but many think that if he does well in the early elections, Iowa and New Hampshire, he may be able to close the gap. If early money is a key predictor of future success, Senator Clinton no longer appears to be the default Democratic nominee that most observers assumed she would be in the beginning of 2007.

A second concern facing Mrs. Clinton's candidacy is the assumption by many that she is simply not electable—while she might be able to win the primary election she will not be able to win the general election against a Republican candidate. Primary voters are typically less moderate (both more liberal and more conservative) than voters in the general election. As a consequence, both parties face the prospect of electing either a more liberal (Democrat) or more conservative (Republican) candidate than is palatable to general-election voters. Thus, while Democratic primary voters may be ready for a woman (not considering the irony that Hillary Clinton is actually among the more conservative of the candidates), the rest of the voting public may not be. One interesting outcome of this fear is the decision by Clinton's campaign office to frequently release polling results, particularly those that place her in a favorable light. Most campaigns avoid doing this on a regular basis for fear that while the outcome may be positive today, it will not be tomorrow, and the campaign will then have to spin the changing results. Hillary Clinton may also face some of the same criticisms that Vice President Al Gore did—that he was too deliberate and too stiff. Clinton, like Gore, has spent numerous years in the spotlight, and perhaps one of the consequences of that attention is a fear of being too genuine. She has had her share of negative press criticizing everything from her hair to her decision to remain in her marriage. As a result, she has become guarded and cool, in contrast to the more dynamic version of herself from her college days. Indeed, her fellow Wellesley classmates remark on her public persona, so different from the "thoughtful friend who called every week after a husband died, or wrote a charming note about the birth of a grandson."[12] Vice President Gore's approach to dealing with his public persona was to switch to more casual clothing, eschewing formal suits for khakis and olive shirts. Time will tell what approach Senator Clinton will take to try to break through the perception of her as aloof.

One way for Mrs. Clinton to soften her image is through her daughter and her husband. The role of Chelsea Clinton is particularly interesting because she is the first child of a president who could potentially have both of her parents serve as president. The Clintons have always maintained a strictly off-limits policy with respect to Chelsea, which the media has generally respected. This was particularly the case for Bill Clinton's first presidential campaign when Chelsea was not yet a teenager. Today, she is 27 and lives and works in Manhattan. Both of her parents have said that the extent to which their daughter wants to become involved in Hillary Clinton's presidential campaign is strictly up to her. Chelsea is an adult now with her own life and interests, and both Bill and Hillary Clinton want to protect her as much as possible from the circus of a presidential election. However, there is speculation that Chelsea Clinton will increase her public role in her mother's campaign as the election draws nearer—this is the approach she took in 2000 when Hillary Clinton ran for the Senate.[13]

Hillary Clinton will also benefit from the presence of her husband, both privately and publicly. Bill Clinton remains very respected, admired, and beloved by much of the American public. Indeed, he continues to enthrall audiences whenever he speaks publicly and is able to raise a constant stream of money by attending a series of fundraisers on behalf of his wife. His role, should Hillary Clinton win the election, is open to considerable speculation. However, he has recently said in a CNN interview that he would plan on not working for any salary so that he would not create any conflict of interest for Mrs. Clinton and that he would be available for whatever she desires. Hillary Clinton, in turn, has suggested that her husband could serve as an ambassador to the world, parlaying his international popularity into a role that would be beneficial to the country. While it is anticipated that Mr. Clinton will not do much public speaking before the fall of 2007, he is clearly a presence behind the scenes. He often reads drafts of his wife's major speeches, provides her with feedback about some of her public events, and discusses strategy with both her and her pollster, Mark Penn.[14] According to two friends, Bill Clinton has said that it is his personal mission to ensure that Mrs. Clinton wins the state of Arkansas, which eluded Vice President Gore in 2000 and Senator Kerry in 2004.[15] According to insiders, Bill Clinton very much wants his wife to succeed in her quest for the presidency and is working very hard to help that come to pass. One of the key differences in her campaign is her decision to treat her husband's accomplishments while president as an asset to her own campaign, unlike Vice President Gore, who opted to minimize his ties to President Clinton (due to the Monica Lewinsky scandal and subsequent impeachment hearings). There is considerable speculation that the decision to keep Bill Clinton under wraps during the 2000 campaign substantially harmed Gore's candidacy. Hillary Clinton is not making the same mistake twice, nor is she repeating the 1992 blunder of claiming that her victory yields a two-for-one deal. Yet she does not shy away from benefiting from Bill Clinton's popularity. However, for all of the considerable benefits that he can bring to her campaign, there are always concerns about the potential pitfalls. His track record indicates the possibility for slipups, but Mrs. Clinton knows how to cut him off when necessary.[16] For now, his role will be to remain in the background so that the public can get to know Mrs. Clinton better. However, he is actively raising money for her and calling in favors to maximize the amount of contributions he can raise on her behalf.[17]

Senator Clinton has another unique challenge that no other candidate for president faces. If she were to win the primary and then the general election, she would represent the continuation of a two-family lock on the presidency creating a dynasty that alternates between the Clinton and Bush families. Indeed, if Hillary Clinton were in office for only one term, that would make 24 years of the presidency shared between the two families. According to *New York Times* editorial columnist, Nicholas Kristof, the very fact that a win by Mrs. Clinton perpetuates the continuation of the two families threatens the democratic nature of the country.[18] While Kristof does not question whether Senator Clinton is a qualified candidate, he argues that all things being equal, it "seems reasonable to count inherited (and wedded) advantage as one factor—and to put a thumb on the scales of those who rose on their own."[19] Not only can one make a case that 24 years of a two-family dynasty fails our notions of an open system where running for election is open to anyone (although the increasing cost of even the lowest level of elections calls into question just how open the system really is), it also creates a dilemma for Hillary Clinton in terms of her strategy when running for office. She simply cannot make a case that she is an outsider or represents change.[20] Indeed, that is part of Barack Obama's attraction for many voters; he represents someone new in the political elite. Candidates often try to distance themselves from Washington when running for office, but the ability to do so credibly is difficult for candidates who embody Washingtonian politics. As someone who has already lived in the White House, Senator Clinton cannot use that approach. She has to cede that niche to Senator Obama. Of course, the fact that Senator Clinton would be the first woman to be president can be considered change.

Further changing the dynamics of the 2008 presidential election will be the changes made by several key states in moving up their primary elections. The U.S. presidential election is unique because candidates must first succeed in their own party primaries and then win the Electoral College vote in the general election. Both of these phases have implications for how presidential elections unfold. Elections are fundamentally a state prerogative, leaving decisions about whether voters must be declared party members in order to vote in the primary and the date of the actual primary election to the state legislatures. However, the national Democratic Party has long declared that there will be no election before the Iowa caucuses and the New Hampshire primary. The order of the subsequent elections is then determined by state legislatures. Having Iowa and New Hampshire first creates interesting logistical and tactical decisions for candidates. Few would argue that Iowa and New Hampshire are the most representative states of the entire nation. The method of campaigning also differs—there is considerable emphasis on retail politicking where candidates spend an inordinate amount of time meeting voters individually, rather than relying on a media campaign. The size of these states, particularly New Hampshire, makes such an approach possible.

Candidates in New Hampshire are expected to go to individual homes and meet voters in small numbers. However, this is considerably more time consuming than using television ads.

Despite the fact that neither Iowa nor New Hampshire is a good microcosm of the larger nation, they play a disproportionate role in influencing the remainder of the primary season. Candidates who do well in either Iowa or New Hampshire can receive a boost that will help their candidacies. This is exactly what occurred in 1992 when then Governor Bill Clinton was running for office. His second-place outcome in the New Hampshire race earned him the label "the comeback kid" and propelled him through the remainder of the election to win the primaries. A poor showing in one of the early states can also spell the demise of a promising candidacy, as was the case with Howard Dean. While many considered him one of the strong front runners in 2004, he did not win in Iowa, and his subsequent reaction (a howl) heard nationwide caused him to ultimately lose all momentum and ultimately the primary election. Presidential elections in the United States often turn on the fickle minds of voters, where an overly emotional outburst can spell the end of a promising candidacy.

In 1988, southern states banded together to create "Super Tuesday" to have a regional impact on the primary elections. All of the southern states decided to hold their primary on the same day early in the calendar year, thereby ensuring that their elections would become a strategic component of the campaigns. This proved particularly useful for President Clinton—being a southerner himself, he was able to take the momentum gained from the surprising second-place result in New Hampshire and parlay that into a win in many of the southern states, which ensured his continued success and eventual nomination.

Realizing the advantage of holding a primary early in the season, several larger states have decided to move up their own primaries for the 2008 presidential election. New York shifted its election so that it would be in the first week of February rather than a month later in March. New York is not alone; it is joined by up to 20 states moving their elections to February 5, which falls a month before the traditional southern Super Tuesday. It is likely that by the end of the day on February 5, the presidential nominees for both parties will have been determined. The regional breadth of these states make the primary a mini national election. The states range from New York to New Mexico, Delaware, California, Connecticut, and Texas. These changes in primary dates place considerable pressure on candidates, creating potential travel, funding, and politicking challenges. Whereas Super Tuesday was limited to one region in the country, the new mini national primary has candidates crisscrossing the nation. Clearly there is considerable expense associated with such travels. However, the breadth of states simultaneously holding elections forces candidates to broaden their message beyond a state-centric focus. Candidates can no longer emphasize only one or two issues important to individual states but need to create a message that appeals to voters across regional lines.

Endorsements are another important component for a successful election. Conventional wisdom has long put Hillary Clinton as the front runner for winning the 2008 Democratic presidential nomination. However, that success requires solid support from the African American community. Both Bill and Hillary Clinton have fared particularly well with black voters, and both can certainly attribute much of their electoral success to that support. However, with Senator Barack Obama in the field and doing well, that automatic support may not be as forthcoming as once assumed. In an April 2007 *New York Times* article, there is considerable discussion about the difficulties facing many black leaders about whom they should endorse for president.[21] Many are starting to view Senator Obama as a truly viable candidate despite his paucity of years in office. As a result, some political leaders who probably could have been counted on to endorse Senator Clinton are now hesitating to do so. They feel an obligation to her; however, they are excited at the prospect of an African American candidate who may have the ability to actually win the nomination.[22] Part of Senator Obama's perceived viability is the amount of money he has raised from such a large number of donors. Winning endorsements will further his potential for success. This in turn places a greater burden on the Clinton campaign to sew up those endorsements that were formerly assumed to be in place, which will have implications for where Hillary Clinton allocates her resources for campaigning. If the African American community begins to show signs of supporting Obama, Senator Clinton will need to expend resources, both time and money, to shore up what she may have taken for granted. This reality may pull her away from winning over other groups necessary for a victory.

The desire for the black vote is not limited to Clinton and Obama. In the beginning of May 2007, all of the Democratic candidates attended the National Conference of Black Mayors. The Black vote is critical for Democratic nominees. Indeed, President Clinton can attribute much of his success in 1992 and 1996 to the solid support of the African American vote. While not homogeneous, blacks continue to vote overwhelmingly Democratic. The key ingredient then is turnout. If African Americans vote, they can make a difference in the outcome of an election. It is thus necessary for all of the Democratic candidates to court the leaders of the black community in order to try to gain support for their nomination.

While there are many elements of running for office that remain unchanged over time, technology has introduced some innovations. Perhaps the greatest change is the use of the Internet. The field of candidates running in the 2008 election is not the first to use the Internet in campaigning, but the Internet is clearly more prevalent today than it was even four years ago. Moreover, the advances in Web sites such as YouTube.com introduce unique opportunities and challenges for candidates. Any speech or activity can be captured and uploaded to the Internet for instantaneous viewing, and anyone can create a spoof of a candidate and upload it. A simple search of Hillary Clinton on Youtube.com yields literally pages and pages of clips. Some are clearly legitimate clips of speeches she has made; others are more dubious. The challenge this presents to Hillary Clinton, and any other candidate running for office, is the loss of control over the message. Candidates running for office strive to shape the way in which they are portrayed by the media. One method for doing so is for the candidates to stay on message and dictate the news that is available for coverage. With the onset of the Internet, this becomes increasingly difficult.

While the Internet presents challenges for the candidates, it also allows them to show their sense of humor. That is certainly the case for Hillary Clinton. Her presidential campaign Web site (http://www.hillaryclinton.com) is currently showing a video of her asking, in very serious tones, for assistance from the American public on an issue that is of critical important to her campaign—selecting a theme song for her campaign. Senator Clinton further spoofs herself by promising not to sing the selected song and a brief clip of her singing the National Anthem—poorly—is shown. Such tactics take advantage of new technology, appeal to younger voters who enjoy going online and participating in interactive Web sites, and also manage to make Hillary Clinton seem more approachable by showcasing her sense of humor. On completion of the poll, Hillary and Bill Clinton used YouTube.com again to do a spoof of *The Sopranos* series finale to announce the winner of the campaign theme song (Celine Dion's "You and I"), again appealing to popular culture as a mechanism to lighten up Hillary Clinton's image.

Regardless of the ultimate outcome of either the primary or general elections, Hillary Clinton has already made history. She is the first First Lady to become a U.S. senator, and she is arguably the first woman to be considered a viable candidate to become president. Given that one of her earliest ambitions of becoming an astronaut was denied due to her sex, she has come a long way in shaping the attitudes and expectations of what women can accomplish. While there may always be speculation about the nature of her relationship with her husband, there is no doubt that Hillary Rodham Clinton is well on the path to realizing her own ambitions.

NOTES

1. "Women Presidential and Vice Presidential Candidates," CAWP Presidential Watch. http://www.cawp.rutgers.edu/Facts/CanHistory/prescand.pdf.

2. Jonathan Alter, "Is America Ready?" *Newsweek*, December 25, 2006, pp. 28–40.

3. Patrick Healy, "Clinton Says 'I'm in to Win' 2008 Race," *New York Times*, January 20, 2007.

4. Ibid.

5. Ivins, Molly, "America Doesn't Need Republican-lite," *Charleston Gazette* (West Virginia), January 23, 2006, p. 14A.

6. Michael Crowley, "Hillary's War," *The New Republic*, April 2, 2007.

7. Matthew Continetti, "Hillary's War: The Loneliness of the Long-Distance Front-Runner," *Weekly Standard*, January 22, 2007.

8. Michael Crowley, "Hillary's War," *The New Republic*, April 2, 2007.

9. Patrick Healy, "Mindful of Past, Clinton Cultivates the Military," *New York Times*, March 27, 2007.

10. Matt Bai, "Mrs. Triangulation," *New York Times Magazine*, October 2, 2005.

11. Patrick Healy and Jeff Zeleny, "Clinton Enters '08 Field, Fueling Race for Money," *New York Times*, January 20, 2007.

12. Tamar Lewin, "Wellesley Class Sees 'One of Us' Bearing Standard," *New York Times*, April 14, 2007.

13. Beth Fouhy, "First Kid Now All Grown Up—Chelsea Ponders Her Role in Mum's Presidential Campaign," *The Courier Mail*, May 15, 2007.

14. Patrick Healy, "In New Role, Senator Clinton's Chief Strategist," *New York Times*, May 13, 2007.

15. Ibid.

16. Ibid.

17. Ibid.

18. Nicholas Kristof, "All in the Families," *New York Times*, May 7, 2007.

19. Ibid.

20. William Kristol, "The 2008 Formula," *Time*, May 14, 2007, p. 33.

21. Raymond Hernandez, "Obama's Rise Strains Loyalty on Clinton Turf," *New York Times*, April 24, 2007.

22. Ibid.

EPILOGUE

SUMMER 2007

By the middle of summer 2007, the 2008 presidential campaign is in full swing, and despite the very early start for the campaigns (January 2007), there seems to be relatively little voter backlash. Instead, voter interest remains at a surprisingly high level. This may be due to the fact that the race remains wide open in both political parties. Although Hillary Clinton may be considered the front runner for the Democrats she has by no means secured her place as the eventual nominee. Likewise, there is no clear front runner in the Republican party. In fact, there have been relatively more changes and surprises among the Republicans than the Democrats.

John McCain, a strong contender in the 2000 election, finds himself in the unusual position of struggling behind his Republican colleagues. Indeed, problems have plagued his campaign almost from the beginning. In particular, he has had difficulty raising sufficient funds and even went so far as to fire his top campaign staffers in early July as a means of shaking up his organization to try to find a way back into the race. In addition to financial difficulties, McCain and the other Republican candidates have had to contend with the possible entrance of Fred Thompson, a popular actor with considerably more traditional Republican values than the other candidates in the party. Thompson clearly benefits from his long run on the hit television show *Law and Order* for name recognition and visibility.

Among the Democrats, Senator Barack Obama continues to thrive in his bid for the nomination. His surprising financial success in the first quarter of 2007 persisted into the second quarter when he reported raising another $31 million, $10 million more than Hillary Clinton's campaign. Unlike many of his fellow candidates, Obama continues to rely on small donations from many individuals. Obama, more than any of his fellow candidates, is successfully using the Internet and small ticket events as a means of increasing the number of donors to his campaign. While the actual amount of money he has raised is impressive, the number of contributors continues to grow at an equally impressive rate. Obama has taken a new approach to relying on supporters to bundle contributions. The Obama campaign has 9,500 volunteers who have agreed to solicit their friends and families to donate to the campaign.[1] Although the amount of money is considerably smaller than the traditional approach to bundling donations, the hope is that those who give now will be more likely to give larger contributions when (and if) the campaign goes up against a Republican nominee. Obama has also spoken at many small money events where the cost to attend is about a $25 donation rather than the more typical multi-hundred dollar donation. Obama is not the only one using new techniques for raising money. John Edwards collects cell phone numbers so that he can text supporters about upcoming events. Edwards's staffers have also appeared on YouTube attempting to make a pecan pie (using Edwards's mother's recipe). Supporters could buy the recipe for $6.10. This campaign raised nearly $300,000 in one week.[2] Given the very low cost of doing the video (buying pie ingredients) the profit was substantial.

Money continues to be of fundamental importance for all of the campaigns, and the success of Senator Obama in raising more than Hillary Clinton clearly secures his place as an ongoing threat to the success of her candidacy. While she may be able to tap into the Democratic establishment more readily than Obama, the fact remains that Obama has outpaced Clinton at bringing new supporters into the campaign and raising money. While Internet success at this stage does not necessarily translate into ultimate success (Howard Dean fared very well on the Internet until his campaign crashed in burned in Iowa in 2004), Barack Obama remains a very real competitor to Hillary Clinton. And one cannot push aside John Edwards. While he has not been nearly as successful as either Obama or Clinton in raising money, Edwards's strength lies in his popularity in Iowa, where the first caucuses will take place. However, a win in Iowa does not automatically translate into success beyond that state.

Among the other challenges facing Hillary Clinton in her bid to be the Democratic nominee is the willingness of voters to elect a woman as president. While she seems to have made some progress in this area, there remains a group of potential voters who are not so sure about a female president, or at least about Mrs. Clinton becoming president. Interestingly, while women remain overall more positive about Hillary Clinton than do men, older and married women are somewhat skeptical about her.[3] This is both good and bad news. There are more women than men in the country and the gender gap typically favors Democratic candidates over Republicans. Although this may prove crucial in the general election, the fact that older and married women are less favorably inclined toward Clinton can spell bad news for the primary election. Interestingly, among those polled, a majority believed that if she were the Democratic nominee, she would win the general election. And Clinton has also made headway into concerns about women and national defense issues with a majority of respondents believing that she would be a successful Commander in Chief.

One of the ongoing balancing acts facing the Clinton campaign is the role of her husband, Bill Clinton. As previously mentioned, it is clearly a unique balancing act that Hillary Clinton strives to master. On one hand, her husband remains extremely popular among Democrats, but that very popularity means that she runs the risk of being overshadowed by his presence. In July 2007 the Clintons campaigned together for the first time in Iowa, a state where she trails former Senator Edwards in every poll. One of the goals of the Clintons is to reverse the pairing of their names; it has always been Bill and Hillary Clinton, but now they are trying to make it Hillary and Bill Clinton to reflect the change in their relative positions. However, it is difficult to reinvent their public image after 15 years in the spotlight. One of the other challenges facing Hillary Clinton's use of her husband in her campaign is that he is simply a more compelling public speaker. While he is working to keep his comments brief, he always manages to give the appearance of intimacy, whereas she generally comes off as stiff and unapproachable.[4] It is clear that the success of Hillary Clinton depends to some extent on her husband, but in the ensuing months it will become more evident whether his role will continue to expand or remain behind the scenes, where there is less risk of stealing the show.

As the campaign continues to move forward, candidates from both parties are engaging in political debates. One of the most interesting formats used for the first time in presidential-election history used questions asked by voters who submitted videos on YouTube.com. CNN sponsored and moderated the debate and the questions ranged across a variety of topics; some even managed to elicit what appeared to be unscripted answers. Nevertheless, most of the candidates fell back on tried and true responses. Perhaps the most interesting fallout from the July 2007 Democratic debate was the beginning of what appears to be a break from civility between Clinton and Obama. The candidates were asked if they would promise to meet with controversial foreign leaders from nations such as Cuba, Venezuela, and Syria during their first year as president. Obama said he would be willing to make such a promise because he thought it was important to maintain open channels of communication with any willing participant. In contrast, Clinton said she would not make such a promise because it would first be important to understand the agenda of the other players before making such a commitment. The next day, Clinton released a statement accusing Obama of being "irresponsible and frankly naïve"[5] demonstrating his lack of experience in national security issues. Obama immediately fired back by saying that Clinton's response was very similar to that of the Bush administration's position on meeting with so-called rogue-state leaders. The gloves appear to be coming off.

As the presidential campaign continues to unfold, it is becoming increasingly clear that Mrs. Clinton maintains her status as a truly viable candidate. However, it is also apparent that Senator Obama is not just a flash-in-the-pan but a real threat to Hillary's chances at winning the nomination. The contest within the Democratic party appears to be focusing increasingly on the two senators. Each is capable of raising considerable sums of money and each brings a vastly different set of credentials and advantages to the table. Senator Obama is seen as the outsider with the fresh ideas and new approach to governing. Clinton has on her side experience, her husband, and the novelty of being a woman candidate. The ensuing months promise to be exciting and intriguing new precedents continue to be set for presidential politics.

NOTES

1. Karen Tumulty, "Obama's Viral Marketing Plan," *Time*, July 16, 2007, pp. 38–39.

2. Ibid.

3. Katharine Q. Seelye and Dalia Sussman, "Women Supportive but Skeptical about Clinton, Poll Says," *New York Times*, July 20, 2007.

4. Mark Halperin, "On the Road Again," *Time*, July 16, 2007, pp. 32–35.

5. Patrick Healy, "Clinton and Obama Campaigns Spar over Debate," *New York Times*, July 26, 2007.

BIBLIOGRAPHY

Alter, Jonathan. "Is America Ready?" *Newsweek*, December 25, 2006, pp. 28–40.

Babcock, Charles, and Sharon LaFraniere. "The Clinton's Finances: A Reflection of Their State's Power Structure," *The Washington Post*, July 21, 1992, p. A7.

Bai, Matt. "Mrs. Triangulation," *New York Times Magazine*, October 2, 2005, p. 62.

Ball, Karen. "Matters of Principle," *The Washington Post*, November 23, 1997, p. W19.

Beschloss, Michael R. *The Impeachment and Trial of President Clinton*. New York: Times Books, Random House, 1999.

Benac, Nancy. "Hillary Clinton's Life of Improbable Turns Pivots Again," *Associated Press*, January 21, 2007.

Brock, David. *The Seduction of Hillary Rodham*. New York: The Free Press, 1996.

Bruck, Conne, and Anita Kunz. "The Politics of Perception," *The New Yorker*, October 9, 1995, p. 50–78.

Burger, Timothy J. "Health Panel Seen for Hil," *Daily News* (New York), January 11, 2001.

"Central America Gets More Help," *Miami Herald*, November 17, 1998, p. A24.

Clinton, Hillary Rodham. *Living History*. New York: Simon and Schuster, 2003.

Clinton, Hillary Rodham. *It Takes a Village: And Other Lessons Children Teach Us*. New York: Simon and Schuster, 1996.

Cobb, Nathan. "The Hillary Jokes—Not Everyone Is Laughing," *The Boston Globe*, April 6, 1993, p.1.

Cohn, Jonathan. "The Health Care Plan That Dare Not Speak its Name," *The New Republic*, June 4, 2007, p. 24–28.

Continetti, Matthew. "Hillary's War: The Loneliness of the Long-Distance Front-Runner," *The Weekly Standard*, January 22, 2007.

Crowley, Michael. "Hillary's War: The Real Reason She Won't Apologize," *The New Republic*, April 2, 2007, p. 19–25.

Dionne, E. J., Jr. "Clinton Traces His Decision Not to Run for President to Family Obligations," *New York Times*, August 16, 1987.

Dowd, Maureen. "Hillary Clinton Says She Once Tried to Be Marine," *New York Times*, June 15, 1994, p. B8.

Drew, Elizabeth. *On the Edge: The Clinton Presidency*. New York: Simon and Shuster, 1995.

Fenno, Richard F. Jr. *Home Style: House Members in Their Districts*. Boston: Little, Brown and Company, 1978.

Fouhy, Beth. "First Kid Now All Grown Up—Chelsea Ponders Her Role in Mum's Presidential Campaign," *The Courier Mail* (Australia), May 15, 2007.

France-Presse, Agence. "Hillary Clinton Supports a Palestinian State," *New York Times*, May 7, 1998, p. A8.

Goldman, Erik L. "Sen. Clinton Eyes EMRs as New Key to Reform: 10 Years Later," *Family Practice News* 34, no. 6 (March 15, 2004): 4–6.

Graber, Doris. *Mass Media and American Politics*, 7th ed. Washington D.C.: CQ Press, 2006.

Green, Joshua. "Take Two: How Hillary Clinton Turned Herself into the Consummate Washington Player," *The Atlantic Monthly*, November 2006.

Halperin, Mark. "On the Road Again," *Time*, July 16, 2007, pp. 32–35.

Harpaz, Beth J. *The Girl's in the Van: A Reporter's Diary of the Campaign Trail*. New York: Thomas Dunne Books, 2001.

Harris, John F. "First Lady Still Interpreting Her Role," *The Washington Post*, November 27, 1996, p. A1.

Healy, Patrick. "Clinton and Obama Campaigns Spar over Debate," *New York Times*, July 26, 2007.

Healy, Patrick. "Clinton Says 'I'm in to Win' 2008 Race," *New York Times*, January 20, 2007.

Healy, Patrick. "Mindful of Past, Clinton Cultivates the Military," *New York Times*, March 27, 2007.

Healy, Patrick. "In New Role, Senator Clinton's Chief Strategist," *New York Times*, May 13, 2007.

Healy, Patrick, and Jeff Zeleny. "Clinton Enters '08 Field, Fueling Race for Money," *New York Times*, January 20, 2007.

Hernandez, Raymond. "Obama's Rise Strains Loyalty on Clinton Turf," *New York Times*, April 24, 2007.

Ivins, Molly, "America Doesn't Need Republican-lite," *Charleston Gazette* (West Virginia), January 23, 2006, p. 14A.

Jakes, Lara. "Clinton Targets Upstate Recovery," *The Times Union* (Albany, NY), November 9, 2000.

Johnson, Paul. H. "Blacks Plan to Watch the Winners They Backed," *The Record* (Troy, NY), November 9, 2000.

Jones, Charles O. "Campaigning to Govern: The Clinton Style." In *The Clinton Presidency*, ed. Colin Campbell and Bert A. Rockman. New Jersey: Chatham House Publishers, 1996.

Just, Marion. "Candidate Strategies and the Media Campaign." In *The Election of 1996: Reports and Interpretations*, ed. Gerald Pomper. New Jersey: Chatham House, 1996.

Kaplan, Fred. "Election 2000: Clinton Wins Seat in Senate," *The Boston Globe*, November 8, 2000.

Keeter, Scott. "Public Opinion and the Election." In *The Election of 1996: Reports and Interpretations*, ed. Gerald Pomper. New Jersey: Chatham House, 1996.

Kennedy, Helen. "60's Turmoil Turns Scholar into Rebel." *New York Daily News*, February 26, 2000, p. 26.

Kennedy, Helen. "The Girl Who Became Hillary, " *New York Daily News*, February 6, 2000, p. 24.

Kingdon, John W. "Models of Legislative Voting," *The Journal of Politics* (August 1977): 563–95.

Kornblut, Anne E., and Jeff Zeleny. "Clinton Won Easily, but Bankroll Shows the Toll," *New York Times*, November 21, 2006.

Kristof, Nicholas. "All in the Families," *New York Times*, May 7, 2007.

Lammers, William W., and Michael Genovese. *The Presidency and Domestic Policy: Comparing Leadership Styles, FDR to Clinton*. Washington D.C.: CQ Press, 2000.

Levy, Dena, and Charles Tien. "Clinton Defeats Lazio in New York's Senate Race." In *The Roads to Congress*, ed. Sunil Ahuja and Robert Dewhirst. New York: Wadsworth, 2002.

Lewin, Tamar. "Wellesley Class Sees 'One of Us' Bearing Standard," *New York Times*, April 14, 2007.

Lippman, Thomas W. "Hillary Clinton Urges Public to Support Foreign Aid," *The Washington Post*, June 17, 1997, p. A13.

Maraniss, David. "Before Race Began, Clinton Pledge Not to Run," *The Washington Post*, July 15, 1992, p. A1.

Maraniss, David. "First Lady of Paradox," *The Washington Post*, January 15, 1995, p. A1.

Matthews, Donald R. *U.S. Senators and Their World*. Westport, Conn.: Greenwood Press, 1980.

Mayhew, David R. *Congress: The Electoral Connection*. New Haven, Conn.: Yale University Press, 1974.

McCaffrey, Shannon. "Hillary Clinton's First 100 Days: Small Victories for a Big Celebrity," *The Associated Press*, April 11, 2001.

McGrory, Mary. "Mr. and Mrs. Comeback Kid, " *The Washington Post*, November 8, 1998, p. C1.

Milton, Joyce. *The First Partner: Hillary Rodham Clinton*. New York: William Morrow and Company, 1999.

Morris, Dick. "Is Hillary Frightened," *The Hill* (Washington, D.C.), May 2, 2001.

Morris, Vincent. "Hill's New Bills Would Boost N.Y.," *The New York Post*, March 2, 2001.

New York Times, "The New York Senate Race," editorial, October 15, 2006.

New York Times, "Most Expensive Races of 2006," November 14, 2006.

Parry-Giles, Shawn. "Mediating Hillary Rodham Clinton: Television News Practices and Image-Making in the Postmodern Age." *Critical Studies in Media Communication* 17, no. 2 (June 2000): 205–26.

Purdum, Todd S. "Mrs. Clinton Forsees Role in Welfare Overhaul," *New York Times*, November 25, 1996, p. A12.

Quirk, Paul J., and Joseph Hichliffe. "Domestic Policy: The Trials of a Centrist Democracy." In *The Clinton Presidency*, ed. Colin Campbell and Bert A. Rockman. New Jersey: Chatham House Publishers, 1996.

Renshon, Stanley A. *High Hopes: The Clinton Presidency and the Politics of Ambition*. New York: Routledge, 1998.

Rodham, Hillary. "Children Under the Law." *Harvard Educational Review* 43 (1973): 487–514.

Santora, Marc. "Clinton Gains Second Term Easily, with Support Extending across Much of the State," *New York Times*, November 8, 2006.

Santora, Marc. "A Gap Never Closed," *New York Times*, November 7, 2006.

Santora, Marc. "Who Cares About the Issues: Is That Botox," *New York Times*, October 26, 2006.

Seelye, Katherine Q. "Hillary Clinton Begins Drive to Improve Care for Children," *New York Times*, October 1, 1997, p. A20.

Seelye, Katharine Q., and Dalia Sussman. "Women Supportive but Skeptical about Clinton, Poll Says," *New York Times*, July 20, 2007.

Sheehy, Gail. *Hillary's Choice*. New York: Random House, 1999.

Sherrill, Martha. "The Education of Hillary Clinton," *The Washington Post*, January 13, 1993, p. D1.

Sherrill, Martha. "The Rising Lawyer's Detour to Success," *The Washington Post*, January 12, 1993, p B1.

Sinclair, Barbara. "Trying to Govern Positively in a Negative Era." In *The Clinton Presidency*, ed. Colin Campbell and Bert A. Rockman. New Jersey: Chatham House Publishers, 1996.

Smith, Chris. "The woman in the Bubble: After Years of Public Trauma, Hillary Clinton Is Secure, Triumphant, Joyous Even. Is it Worth Giving up

All That for the White House?" *New York Magazine*, November 13, 2006, p. 30–39.

Sonner, Molly W., and Clyde Wilcox. "Forgiving and Forgetting: Public Support for Bill Clinton during the Lewinsky Scandal, " *PS: Political Science and Politics* 32, no. 3 (September 1999): 554–57.

Tien, Charles, Regan Checchio, and Arthur H. Miller. "The Impact of First Wives on Presidential Campaigns and Elections." In *Women in Politics: Outsiders or Insiders*, 3rd ed., ed. Lois Duke-Whitaker. New Jersey: Prentice Hall, 1999.

Toobin, Jeffrey. *A Vast Conspiracy*. New York: Random House, 2000.

Tumulty, Karen. "Obama's Viral Marketing Plan," *Time*, July 16, 2007, pp. 38–39.

Warner, Judith. *Hillary Clinton: The Inside Story*. New York: Penguin Books, 1993.

Watson, Robert P. "Source Material: Toward the Study of the First Lady: The State of Scholarship," *Presidential Studies Quarterly* 33, no. 2 (June 2003): 423–41.

Wayne, Stephen J. *The Road to the White House, 1996*. New York: Simon and Shuster, 1997.

Wayne, Stephen J., G. Calvin Mackenzie, and Richard L. Cole. *Conflict and Consensus in American Politics.* Belmont, Calif.: Thomson Wadsworth, 2007.

Wilson, Graham K. "The Clinton Administration and Interest Groups." In *The Clinton Presidency*, ed. Colin Campbell and Bert A. Rockman. New Jersey: Chatham House Publishers, 1996.

Woodward, Bob. *The Agenda: Inside the Clinton White House*. New York: Simon and Schuster, 1994.

WEBSITES

Center for American Women and Politics (CAWP) official Web site: http://www.cawp.rutgers.edu.

Clinton Presidential Materials Project. The National Archives: http://clinton6.nara.gov.

GovTrack: http://www.govtrack.us.

Hillary For President. Hillary Clinton for President Exploratory Committee. http://www.hillaryclinton.com.

MSNBC News: http://www.msnbc.msn.com.

Source Watch: A Project of the Center for Media and Democracy: http://www.sourcewatch.org.

Wellesley College official Web site: http://www.wellesley.edu, accessed 4/30/2007

USEFUL WEB SITES FOR FURTHER RESEARCH

There are many Web sites available today that are useful sources for tracking information about the legislative activities of any elected official. Although information in this book is only current as of May 2007, those interested in pursuing the legislative activities of Senator Clinton can do so quite easily.

www.thomas.gov.

> This Web site is maintained by the Library of Congress. It contains a wealth of information about all levels of government. Researchers can locate what bills a member has sponsored and cosponsored, the voting record of any given legislative session, text of bills, and remarks made in the *Congressional Record*. In addition, one can track the path of any legislation to determine whether it has been reported out of committee, marked up, and so on. One of the obvious strengths of this particular site is that it is a service of the Library of Congress and is comprised of original sources. There is a lot of information available for any interested researcher and links provide general information the House, the Senate, and other parts of government.

www.govtrack.us.

> This is an independent Web site that allows researchers to track legislative progress, voting records of members of Congress, and other such data. This site will also provide e-mail updates about areas of interest. GovTrack compiles data from www.thomas.gov and other Web sites and provides summary information about individual members' legislative activities. One of the unique components of this site is that it will provide comparative information about members of Congress. For example, it will provide the number of bills sponsored in relationship to other members—whether average, above average, or below average. A researcher can also learn about the status of legislation, the voting record of an individual member, and biographical data.

www.votesmart.org.

> Project Vote Smart is a unique organization that strives to provide information about any elected candidate (and those running for office) in the most transparent way possible. A nonprofit organization where the majority of staff are volunteers, Project Vote Smart does not accept any funding from corporations, interest groups, or PACs. The mission of the organization is to provide voters with "access to abundant, accurate and relevant information." The hope is that by so doing, power will be returned to voters and the ability of candidates and elected officials to manipulate information will be minimized. One of the hallmarks of this organization is the diversity

of its board members. All views are represented to ensure that the pluralist nature of democracy is maintained. The Web site provides researchers with information about voting records, interest group ratings, issue positions, campaign finances, and public statements. In addition the site provides information on other governmental aspects such as the judiciary, voter registration, polling places, and links for state-level information.

www.opensecrets.org.

This Web site is sponsored by the Center for Responsive Politics, which is a nonprofit, nonpartisan research organization. The Center's focus is money in elections and how that effects public policy. Candidates running for office are required to disclose their contributors and this site provides access to that information for the general public. A researcher can thus easily determine who gives to whom, and how much.

www.opencongress.org.

Sponsored by the Sunlight Foundation (which seeks to provide transparency to the governmental system, www.sunlightfoundation.com) Open Secrets is another Web site much in the same vein as those previously mentioned. However, while it does provide data about pending legislation and elected officials, it also incorporates blogs to give the stories behind the bills. While the data are reliable it should be remembered that blog submissions are purely the opinions of the writers. Nevertheless, this site does have a unique niche in the list of resources available for conducting research.

www.senate.gov.

This is the official Web site of the United States Senate (there is a parallel one for the House of Representatives, www.house.gov) where senators maintain their official Web sites. Senator Clinton's Web site is http://clinton.senate.gov/ and it provides considerable information about her activities on behalf of her constituents. Senator Clinton has a separate Web site for her presidential campaign: www.hillaryclinton.com. Here, one can research Clinton's positions on a vast array of issues, watch a video clip made by former President Clinton about his wife's strengths as a presidential candidate, and contribute money to her campaign.

HILLARY CLINTON'S PUBLICATIONS

Living History. New York: Simon and Schuster, 2004.

An Invitation to the White House: At Home with History. New York: Simon and Schuster, 2000.

This book provides an insider's view of the White House and its place in American culture. The book includes numerous photographs to bring to life the various steps that go into planning State dinners, the annual Easter egg roll, and other activities that occur behind the scenes at the White House.

Dear Socks, Dear Buddy : Kids' Letters to the First Pets. New York: Simon and Schuster, 1998.

This book was written while Hillary Clinton was First Lady. She shares anecdotes and details about the "First Pets": Socks and Buddy. She encourages parents to help their children write letters as a means of communication. She also shares some of the letters that Socks and Buddy received while in office.

It Takes a Village : And Other Lessons Children Teach Us. New York: Simon and Schuster. 1996.

In this book, Hillary Clinton focuses on her passion: children. Clinton examines other nations and how they raise children as a point of comparison to the United States in order to determine what kinds of changes can and ought to be made for American children to flourish.

INDEX

ABOUT THE AUTHORS

DENA B. LEVY is associate professor of political science at State University of New York Brockport. She has published widely on women, gender, and minority issues in politics.

NICOLE R. KRASSAS is associate professor of political science and women's studies at Eastern Connecticut State University. Her primary scholarly areas of interest are gender and mass mediated rhetoric.